The Divine Glory of Christ

CHARLES J. BROWN

The Banner of Truth Trust

THE BANNER OF TRUTH TRUST
3 Murrayfield Road, Edinburgh EH 12 6EL
PO Box 621, Carlisle, Pennsylvania 17013, USA

FIRST PUBLISHED 1868
FIRST BANNER OF TRUTH TRUST EDITION 1982
ISBN 0 85151 342 5
Set in 11 on 12½pt Plantin VIP
and printed and bound in England by
Hazell Watson & Viney Ltd
Aylesbury, Bucks

PREFACE

MY design, in this little volume, has been to accomplish two objects in combination – first, to contribute somewhat that might not be altogether without value, theologically, in the Socinian and some other controversies; and, second, so to do this as to promote at the same time the edification of the devout reader. With respect to the former object, I am of course aware that there is nothing new in the mere general idea of *indirect or incidental testimonies* of Scripture to the Divinity of Christ. But I have at least attempted to examine this department of proof with care; to arrange and classify those testimonies which have long, in my own reading of Scripture, seemed to me of most weight and interest; and, altogether, to give to this species of evidence a more prominent place than has for the most part been assigned to it. The thoughts in the second chapter, and more or less thereafter, on the bearing of the *unity* of God as taught in Scripture on the proof of the Saviour's Divinity, will not, so far as I am aware, be found elsewhere, and have for many years appeared to me to possess considerable importance, theologically and controversially. Then, I am very hopeful, as respects the second object – that of the Christian reader's edification – that I have not here entirely missed the mark. I think that, among other things, he will find not a few passages of the Word of God presented in lights and bearings somewhat fresh, and fitted to draw from the heart such utterances as these, 'My beloved is white and ruddy; the chiefest among ten thousand' – 'Whom have I in heaven but thee? and there is none upon earth that I desire beside thee' – 'Thy words were found, and I did eat them; and thy word was unto me the joy and rejoicing of my heart.' In both views, the theological and the practical, I desire humbly to commend these pages to the blessing of Him of whose transcendent beauty and glory I have briefly written.

C. J. B.

EDINBURGH, *November 1867.*

CONTENTS

———

Contents

CHAPTER 5

CHAPTER 6

INTRODUCTION

LET those great words of the Lord Jesus be recalled to mind – 'O Jerusalem, Jerusalem, thou that killest the prophets, and stonest them which are sent unto thee, how often would I have gathered thy children together, even as a hen gathereth her chickens under her wings, and ye would not.' The bearing of these words on the *character* of Jesus is very obvious, – on his grace especially – his deep, wondrous compassion. It is not quite so obvious that they have a mighty bearing also, and none the less important that it is indirect and incidental, on the glory of the Saviour's *Person*. 'I would have gathered thy children together,' said he, addressing the city of Jerusalem. Of course, by Jerusalem's children he meant her people at large. It is computed that the inhabitants of Jerusalem at that time must have been about a million souls. 'I would have gathered them under my wing,' said Jesus Christ, even as a hen gathereth her little brood of chickens under hers! What manner of man is this – a million souls gathered beneath his wing? It *can* be none other than he of whom David sang, 'He that dwelleth in the secret place of the Most High shall abide under the shadow of the Almighty. He shall cover thee

with his feathers, and under his wings shalt thou trust.'
Why, no human mind is able even to conceive distinctly
what a million *is*. Our ideas have become wholly vague
and undefined long before we have reached that sum.
Who is this that speaks of gathering all the souls in the
city of Jerusalem beneath his wing, keeping them secure
there to eternity, and with as much ease as a hen gathers
her half-dozen chickens under hers? Who but he of
whom Moses sang, 'As an eagle stirreth up her nest,
fluttereth over her young, spreadeth abroad her wings,
taketh them, beareth them on her wings, so the Lord
alone did lead him, and there was no strange God with
him,' – He of whom Boaz said to Ruth, 'The Lord
recompense thy work, and a full reward be given thee of
the Lord God of Israel, under whose wings thou art come
to trust' – that very God, now manifest in the flesh, and
about to 'purchase the Church with his own blood?'

Well; let this example suffice to indicate generally the
field which is contemplated in these pages. It is the field,
mainly, of *indirect or incidental testimonies of Scripture to
the supreme Divinity of Christ*. Those testimonies which
are more express and direct are usually arranged under
such heads as the following – the names and most peculiar titles of God given to Christ; the whole attributes and
perfections of Deity ascribed to him; the highest and
most characteristic works of God declared to be *his*
works; and the highest worship of God on earth and in
heaven rendered to him. Of course, these are the most
obvious sources of proof. Nor need I say that I entertain
no shadow of doubt that the proof from any one of them,
and much more from all together, is complete and irre-

fragable. At the same time it cannot fail to be alike interesting and profitable, if we shall find this grand and fundamental truth of Scripture – the key-stone of the Bible – receiving confirmations from many a quarter where we might less have expected them; if we shall find that we are not obliged to build our faith of the Saviour's Divinity even on some fifty, sixty, seventy, or a hundred passages, where it is directly affirmed and taught; but that it runs as a golden thread throughout the entire Scriptures, and many a time is taught even more powerfully, by being taken for granted – evidently assumed and pre-supposed.

I hope, before the close, to indicate several great uses, apart from the matter of *proof* – uses alike doctrinal and practical – of those incidental testimonies to the divine glory of Christ which are to engage our attention. For the present I content myself with marking only one. It will be found that not a few of our indirect testimonies occur in places of Scripture where the most *obvious* idea, the one which lies on the face of the passage, is not the glory, but the grace, not the majesty but the mercy, of the Saviour. And thus we are exceedingly apt, taken up with the grace which lies on the surface, to overlook the glory, the majesty, that lies beneath – a mistake the more unhappy and injurious on this account, that the very *grace* in such passages is never to be seen in its highest emphasis and excellency, till it is seen in immediate conjunction with the glory of him whose grace it is; so that, in losing the glory, we lose to a very large extent the grace also. Thus, in our illustrative passage, 'O Jerusalem, Jerusalem, thou that killest the prophets, and stonest them which are sent unto thee, how often would I have gathered thy children together, even as a hen gathereth her chickens under her wings,' the *grace* is evidently the idea that lies on the face of the words – the unspeakable tenderness and compassion of the Saviour – his willingness to have gathered beneath his wing even the killers of the prophets, and the stoners of those which were sent unto them. But how is that compassion, tenderness, grace, enhanced in its character, and in its fitness to draw the confidence of a lost soul, when it is seen in conjunction with the glory; when, in union with all the tenderness of a mother's yearnings over her young, the outstretched wing is beheld in all the grandeur of supreme Divinity – Emmanuel, God manifest in the flesh! Oh, it is the majesty of the wing which gives very much of its excellency to the tenderness and grace of the heart. And thus does it become a matter of the greatest importance to exercise ourselves in the study of all those words of Jesus, where *both* the elements, the glory and the grace, the majesty and the tenderness, appear in wondrous combination. For in that combination there is something singularly fitted, under the teaching of the Holy Ghost, to disarm the soul of all its jealousies and suspicions, and constrain it to exclaim, 'It is the voice of my Beloved', 'Set me as a seal upon thine heart, as a seal upon thine arm', let me be ever in the hands of such an One, in his majesty able, in his ineffable tenderness and grace willing, to meet the case of my soul to the uttermost. 'Lord, I believe; help thou mine unbelief!'

CHAPTER 1

INCIDENTAL TESTIMONIES TO THE DIVINE GLORY OF CHRIST FROM THE CLAIMS OF HIS AUTHORITY.

I. WILL the reader mark those solemn words of the Lord Jesus – 'He that loveth father or mother more than me, is not worthy of me; and he that loveth son or daughter more than me, is not worthy of me.' 'There went great multitudes with him; and he turned, and said unto them, If any man come to me, and hate not his father, and mother, and wife, and children, and brethren, and sisters, yea, and his own life also, he cannot be my disciple.' *Matt* 10:37, compared with *Luke* 14:25, 26.

He that loveth father or mother more than me, is not worthy of me. Behold here a teacher who, utterly unlike all that had come from God before him, claims for *himself* the supreme affection of his disciples; claims, not for another, but for himself, the very throne of their hearts – 'He that loveth father or mother more *than me*, is not worthy of me.' Who is this that commands me to prefer him, in the love of my innermost soul, before my own wife, child, mother, father; yea, requires that, when the claims of their love and of his come into conflict, I must be ready to cast theirs at once behind my back; to treat father, mother, sister, brother, wife, child, as if I hated them, deaf to sobs and entreaties, to authority and arguments, to tears and commands, like one whose commendation was thus written of old, 'Who said unto his father and to his mother, I have not seen them; neither did he acknowledge his brethren, nor knew his own children?'

If Christ be none other than the God of whom it is commanded in the law, 'Thou shalt love the Lord thy God with all thy heart, and soul, and mind, and strength,' then I can understand it at least, however imperfectly able to reach it. Then my whole soul assents to the claim as holy and just and good. Then is it easily understood why it should be written, 'If any man love not the Lord Jesus Christ, let him be Anathema Maranatha; and why, from the judgment seat, it should be made the hinge of our everlasting blessedness or woe – 'ye did it,' or, 'ye did it not, *to me*.' And I can but fall down at his feet under a profound consciousness of shortcoming, and plead with him, O Lord Jesus, circumcise my heart to love thee; give what thou requirest, and require whatsoever thou wilt; entreat me not to leave thee; put thy law, thy love, into my inward parts, and write it in my heart! But if he be *not* the God of the law, the God who made me, and made me for himself, then who is he? What creature is this that bids me prefer him in love before my own wife, before my own children? Can I do it, or ought I? And if I do, if I shall have once given him the throne of my heart, *what other throne shall remain in it* to be afterwards given in obedience to the commandment, 'Thou shalt love the Lord thy God with all thy heart, and soul, and mind, and strength'?

2. Perhaps the same result will come out still more palpably in connection with a second example of the claims of Christ's authority. 'I John saw the holy city, new Jerusalem, coming down from God out of heaven, prepared as a bride adorned for her husband. . . . There came unto me one of the seven angels which had the seven vials full of the seven last plagues, and talked with me, saying, Come hither, I will show thee the bride, the Lamb's wife' (*Rev* 21:2, 9). That is to say, the whole ransomed Church, of every kindred, and tongue, and people, and nation, are even now standing, and are throughout eternity to stand, in the relation of the wedded spouse and wife of the Lord Jesus Christ! Compare with John's words those of Paul, 'I have espoused you to one husband, that I may present you as a chaste virgin to Christ;' and those of John the Baptist, 'Ye yourselves bear me witness, that I said, I am not the Christ, but that I am sent before him. *He that hath the bride is the bridegroom.*'

Let it be remembered that the Old Testament Scriptures were very familiar with a marriage relationship on the part of the Church of God. Thus, it is written in them, 'Thy maker is thine husband; the Lord of hosts is his name.' 'I will betroth thee unto me for ever; yea, I will betroth thee unto me in righteousness.' 'Turn, O backsliding children, saith the Lord, for I am married unto you.' 'Behold, I will hedge up thy way with thorns, and make a wall that she shall not find her paths; and she shall follow after her lovers, but she shall not overtake them; and she shall seek them, but shall not find them: then shall she say, I will

go and return to my first husband; for then was it
better with me than now.' O yes, for the whole
iniquities of the ancient Church together are again and
again reduced to this one head, this one capital charge,
of spiritual adultery, – giving the heart to other lovers,
no matter who or what they might happen to be, than
the one husband, Jehovah.

But now, who is this who appears in the New Testament under this very character, claiming it to himself,
and commanding his servants thus to claim it *for* him, 'I
have espoused you to one husband, that I may present
you as a chaste virgin to Christ'; 'He that hath the bride'
(*he that* hath, *alone* hath, right to the innermost heart of
the bride) 'is the bridegroom,' and this to all eternity; 'I
saw a new heaven and a new earth; for the first heaven
and the first earth were passed away. And I John saw the
holy city, new Jerusalem, coming down from God out of
heaven, prepared as a bride adorned for her husband'?
Assuredly, if this be any other than the Jehovah of the
Old Testament, then the religion of the New is by far the
most formidable attack on the God of the Old that was
ever made.

Blessed Jesus, forgive the thought, and teach me
only how to give thee my innermost heart more and
more! 'Tell me, O thou whom my soul loveth, where
thou feedest!' 'Set me as a seal upon thine heart, as a
seal upon thine arm; for love is strong as death, jealousy
is cruel as the grave!' And let me rest thoroughly
assured that, when I shall find at length my very
heaven in thee, my highest good and blessedness,
according to thy words, 'Where I am, there shall also

my servant be', 'Father, I will that they also whom thou hast given me be with me where I am, that they may behold my glory', it shall be in divinest harmony with that appeal to Jehovah, 'Whom have I in heaven *but thee?* and there is none upon earth that I desire beside thee.'

3. As a third example of the claims of Christ's authority, let us take the precious, well-known narrative in *Luke* 7:36, etc.: 'And one of the Pharisees desired him that he would eat with him. And he went into the Pharisee's house, and sat down to meat. And, behold, a woman in the city, which was a sinner, when she knew that Jesus sat at meat in the Pharisee's house, brought an alabaster box of ointment, and stood at his feet behind him weeping, and began to wash his feet with tears, and did wipe them with the hairs of her head, and kissed his feet, and anointed them with the ointment.' The Pharisee believed he had at length fairly detected the falsehood of our Lord's claims. Proceeds the evangelist, 'Now when the Pharisee which had bidden him saw it, he spake within himself, saying, This man, if he were a prophet, would have known who and what manner of woman this is that toucheth him; for she is a sinner.'

The Lord Jesus meets the thought by the following parable and question: 'There was a certain creditor which had two debtors: the one owed five hundred pence, and the other fifty. And when they had nothing to pay, he frankly forgave them both. Tell me therefore, which of them will love him most? Simon answered and said, I suppose that he to whom he forgave most.

[17]

And he said unto him, Thou hast rightly judged. And he turned to the woman, and said unto Simon' — then let the following words be noted with special care – 'Seest thou this woman? I entered into thine house, thou gavest me no water for my feet: but she hath washed my feet with tears, and wiped them with the hairs of her head.' Now every one sees whom the *debtors* here are designed to represent – even the woman, on the one hand, and (with such an allusion to Simon's case as might have shown him his perfect welcome to forgiveness, had he been content to have it on the same footing of absolute grace with this woman whom he scorned) some forgiven sinner of less guilt than hers, upon the other. But is it at all less certain whom the *creditor* represents, who the great Creditor here is, to whom the debt of sin is owing, who alone can remit the debt, and to whom the supreme gratitude and love of the forgiven sinner are due? Let the words be again read, 'He turned to the woman, and said unto Simon, Seest thou this woman? *I* entered into thine house, thou gavest *me* no water for my feet: but she hath washed my feet with tears, and wiped them with the hairs of her head.' Assuredly Jesus at least claims at the hand of Simon, and accepts at the woman's hand, *the love due to the debt-remitting Creditor*. 'Tell me,' was the question, 'which of them will love him [the creditor] most? I suppose that he to whom he forgave most. And he said unto him, Thou hast rightly judged. And he turned to the woman, and said unto Simon, I entered into thine house, thou gavest me no water for my feet; but she hath washed my feet with tears, and wiped them with the hairs of her head. Thou gavest me no kiss; but this woman, since the time I came in, hath not ceased to kiss my feet. My head with oil thou didst not anoint; but this woman hath anointed my feet with ointment. Wherefore I say unto thee, Her sins, which are many, are forgiven; for [that is to say, in evidence whereof] she loved much.'

Loved *whom?* Christ, of course. She had uttered no words, indeed. Her love was too deep for utterance. But she had stood at his feet behind him weeping, and washed his feet with tears, and wiped them with the hairs of her head, and kissed his feet, and anointed them with the ointment. The parable evidently has no meaning, and no application to the matter in hand, unless the love were *given at that table, on the one hand, and withheld, upon the other, from the true and proper creditor.* Jesus Christ, therefore, is the Creditor – the God to whom the debt of all our sin is owing; whose law it is we have broken; who alone can remit our debt; with whom, in the whole matter of sin and its forgiveness, we have to do; and who lays claim to the supreme gratitude and love of every forgiven soul!

There is to my mind something unspeakably sublime about the whole narrative, in this aspect of it. The Pharisee believed, as I have said, that he had at length caught our Lord in his toils, 'This man, if he were a prophet, would have known who and what manner of woman this is that toucheth him; for she is a sinner.' Ah, Simon, not only does he know that well, and that she is a saint also now, but he arraigns thee, suddenly, before his tribunal as the very Creditor and Lord, to whom thou owest all thy debts and duties alike – 'there was a certain creditor which had two debtors. . . . *I* entered into thine house,' etc., etc., It is interesting to compare, in passing, such words elsewhere as these, 'There is one Lawgiver, who is able to save and to destroy', '*Him* with whom we have to do', 'Against thee, thee *only*, have I sinned', 'I, even I, am he that blotteth out thy transgressions.' No doubt there are many other places of the Scripture where both the forgiving of sins by the Lord Jesus, and his receiving the adoration and love of his forgiven people, are more expressly found. But there is something singularly interesting and important in a passage like this, where the whole is quietly assumed and presupposed.

See how the very *quietness* tends to hide the glory from our view. Is not the reason of its being so obvious whom the debtors represent, and so apt to pass unobserved whom the creditor means, partly just the stupendous character of this latter fact, and partly, that stupendous as it is, it is *silently taken for granted throughout?* But what a radiance surrounds the entire narrative, when it is brought out to view! And how precious a confirmation is lent to all more express and direct testimonies of the divine glory of the Saviour, when thus, in places where it is least apt to be thought of, it is found to be so certainly assumed and proceeded upon!

4. Let the parable of the talents, in Matthew chapter 25, be taken for a fourth example of the claims of Christ's authority. Verse 14, 'For the kingdom of heaven is as a man travelling into a far country,

[meaning Christ, I need scarcely say] who called his own servants [all of *us*, for example] and delivered unto them his goods. And unto one he gave five talents, to another two, and to another one' – our time, property, station in life, mental capacities, advantages of every kind. All, then, it seems, are *Jesus Christ's 'his* goods,' and *are given to us by him* – 'He delivered unto them his goods.' And they are given by him to us to be used for him, and accounted for to him. Verse 19, 'After a long time, the lord of those servants cometh, and reckoneth with them. And so he that had received five talents, came and brought other five talents, saying, Lord, thou deliveredst unto me five talents; behold, I have gained beside them five talents more. His lord said unto him, Well done, good and faithful servant.' Thus, as the responsibility for all is to Christ, and the reckoning for all is with Christ, so the everlasting reward also is with and from Christ, 'Well done, good and faithful servant, thou hast been faithful over a few things, I will make thee ruler over many things; enter thou into the joy of thy Lord.' Verse 24, 'Then he which had received the one talent, came and said, Lord, I knew thee that thou art an hard man,' etc. 'And I was afraid, and went and hid thy talent in the earth; lo, there thou hast that is thine. His lord answered and said unto him, Thou wicked and slothful servant' – for now the doom, the final and everlasting punishment also, is from Christ – 'Thou wicked and slothful servant, thou knewest,' etc. 'Cast ye the unprofitable servant into outer darkness, there shall be weeping and gnashing of teeth.'

And then at once without any break, comes the final judgment of the world. 'When the Son of man shall come in his glory, and all the holy angels with him, then shall he sit on the throne of his glory; and before him shall be gathered all nations.' Oh, the eternal divinity of the crucified One, how it shines in the words! The sheep set on his right hand, the goats on his left. 'Come', 'Depart *from me*', 'Ye did it unto *me*', 'Ye did it not to *me*.' How entirely manifest that, if Jesus were not the very and eternal God, then he had, in the whole parable of the talents, and in the whole scene of the judgment, just shifted all human responsibility, duty, service, sin, hope, fear, everlasting destiny, clean off from that God to a creature! Frightful to be even conceived for a moment! 'My Lord and my God!' 'Thy throne, O God, is for ever and ever; the sceptre of thy kingdom is a right sceptre.'

5. I take but one other example from the claims of Christ's authority. 'The love of Christ constraineth us; because we thus judge, that if one died for all, then were all dead' [or rather, died – in him, that is to say], 'and that he died for all, that they which live *should not henceforth live unto themselves, but unto him who died for them, and rose again,*' (2 *Cor* 5:14, 15; compared with *Rom* 14:7-9). 'For none of us liveth to himself, and no man dieth to himself. For whether we live, unto the Lord; and whether we die, we die unto the Lord: whether we live therefore, or die, we are the Lord's. For to this end Christ both died, and rose, and revived, that he might be Lord both of the dead and of the

living.' *That they who live should live unto him who died for them, and rose again.*

Now men may dispute and palter about different kinds of religious worship. Just as the Romanists strive to put a face on their creature worship by attempted distinctions between a higher worship and a lower; so the Socinians, when we point them to such words as these, 'Lord Jesus, receive my spirit!' 'Worthy is the Lamb that was slain, to receive power, and riches, and wisdom, and strength, and honour, and glory, and blessing,' attempt to distinguish between a higher worship given to the Father, and a lower to the Son. We refuse, of course, to admit the plea; we believe it to be entirely groundless and untenable. But let us, for argument's sake, concede it for a moment. *Here* is worship at least, the highest of all worship, than which, whether the knee be bent or not, higher can be rendered to no being – even *'living to him,'* taking his will for our law, himself for our highest good, and end of existence, 'Whether we live, we live unto the Lord' – 'that they who live should live unto him who died for them and rose again.' Or, as Paul elsewhere expresses it with reference to himself, 'To me *to live is Christ.'* If Jesus Christ were not very and eternal God, then, after we had learned to 'live to him,' to take his will for our supreme law, and himself for our highest good and end, what should remain afterwards to be given to the blessed God? What *could* remain but a mockery of worship, no matter by what name it might be called?

I might have multiplied examples much further under this head, noticing, for instance, the words,

'There is one lawgiver, who is able to save and to destroy,' and comparing with it words like these, 'Ye are my friends, if ye do whatsoever I command you'; 'not without law to God, but under law to Christ'; 'bringing every thought into captivity unto the obedience of Christ.' Or I might have taken those words, 'Cursed is the man that trusteth in man, and maketh flesh his arm, and whose heart departeth from the Lord,' and compared with them these, 'Ye believe in God, believe also in me'; 'looking for the mercy of our Lord Jesus Christ unto eternal life'; 'I know whom I have believed, and am persuaded that he is able to keep that which I have committed unto him against that day.' Or I might have noticed the words, 'Thou, even thou, art to be feared,' and compared these with them, 'Kiss the Son, lest he be angry, and ye perish from the way when his wrath is kindled but a little. Blessed are all they that put their trust in him'; 'They shall say to the mountains and rocks, Fall on us, and hide us from the face of him that sitteth upon the throne, and *from the wrath of the Lamb:* for the great day of his wrath is come; and who shall be able to stand?'

In place, however, of enlarging further in this chapter, I would fain ask the reader's attention, in the next one, to a line of thought which has long appeared to my mind of very great moment, in connection with the proper Divine glory of the Saviour. I refer to the bearing of the Scripture doctrine of the Unity of God on the proof of the Saviour's Divinity.

CHAPTER 2

THE BEARING OF THE SCRIPTURE DOCTRINE OF THE DIVINE UNITY ON THE PROOF OF THE SAVIOUR'S DIVINITY.

SOCINIANS are accustomed to claim the name *Unitarian*, as if they alone were the friends of the divine Unity. It has long appeared to my mind that, taking the unity of God, not in any loose, general sense of unity, but as the doctrine is taught throughout the sacred writings, it forms the very source whence the strongest perhaps of all proofs arise of the true and proper Divinity of the Lord Jesus Christ. For, when the Scripture teaches that there is one only God, the meaning will be found to be, not anything of this kind, that there is one Being immeasurably greater, wiser, better, than all others, *but* that there is one Being, besides whom there is in a sense none else at all, a Being of such a sole, unapproached excellency, and glory in all things, in being and in all perfection, that if you would bring any creature into comparison with him – it is a matter of indifference whether it be an archangel or a worm – He stands quite alone, in respect of the one and the other alike. Thus, as to *being*, 'God said unto Moses, I AM THAT I AM; thus shalt thou say unto the children of Israel, I AM hath sent me unto you' (*Exod* 3:14). *I am!* But others also are – are they not? Yes (to use the words of an illustrious writer of the 18th century), 'other things also are, and have been, and shall be. But because what they have been, might have been otherwise; and what they are, might as possibly not have been at all; and what they shall be, may be very different from what now is; therefore of their changeable and dependent essence, which to-day may be one thing, and to-morrow another thing, and the next day possibly nothing at all; of such a changeable and dependent essence, compared with the invariable existence of God, it scarce deserves to be affirmed that it *is*.' But the self-existent God, 'the King eternal, immortal, immortal by an independent, necessary, unchanged existence, influenced by no power, impaired by no time; affected, varied, by no accident, no event whatsoever – is thus fitly described as the I AM. 'I am,' says He, 'and there is none besides me.' 'All nations before Him are as nothing.' 'I AM hath sent me unto you.'

And so, as to perfections, works, glory, worship, we find in Scripture the following momentous words: 'There is none good *but one*, that is God'; 'Thou *only* art holy'; 'The *only* wise God'; 'The blessed and *only* Potentate'; 'Who *only* hath immortality'; 'Who *only* doeth wondrous things'; 'Thou, even thou *only*, knowest the hearts of the children of men'; 'I am the LORD that maketh all things, that stretcheth forth the heavens *alone*, that spreadeth abroad the earth by myself'; 'I kill, and I make alive'; 'I, even I, am Jehovah, and besides me there is no Saviour'; 'There is one Lawgiver, who is able to save and to destroy'; 'Him with whom we have to do'; 'Whom have I in heaven but thee? and there is none upon earth that I desire beside thee'; 'The LORD, whose name is Jealous, is a jealous God'; 'I am Jehovah; that is my name: and my glory will I not give to another'; 'Of him, and through him, and to him, are all things; to whom be glory for ever. Amen.' Such is the Unity of God, as taught in the Scriptures; not the greatest, wisest, best of Beings merely, but, in a sense, the one only Being at all; much as other lights, however useful in the dark, are extinguished in the blazing sun. 'I AM,' – a Being, I repeat, of such sole, unapproached excellency, glory, in all things, that if you would bring any creature into comparison with him, it is of no consequence whether it be an archangel or a worm.

Well; but there walked once on this earth a man, bone of our bone, and flesh of our flesh, of whom it is written, 'To me to live is Christ'; 'Whether we live, we live unto the Lord, and whether we die, we die unto the Lord; whether we live, therefore, or die, we are the Lord's'; 'that they who live should not henceforth live unto themselves, but unto him who died for them, and rose again'; not to speak of words like those, 'Before Abraham was, I am'; 'I am Alpha and Omega, the first and the last'; 'I am the resurrection and the life'; 'All things were created by him, and for him'; 'all the churches shall know that I am he which searcheth the reins and hearts'; 'Worthy is the Lamb that was slain, to receive power, and riches, and wisdom, and strength, and honour, and glory, and blessing'; 'To him that loved us, and washed us from our sins in his own blood, be glory and dominion for ever and ever.'

If the unity of God were nothing more than some immeasurable superiority over all other Beings, then, for aught I know, such things *might* be spoken of one who after all was not Jehovah, but only some creature near him in the scale of being? But, near to *Him* in the scale of being? The thing is an impossibility. And the instant it has been seen as such, and cast out as a blasphemy, the instant the unity of Jehovah has been grasped as importing such an aloneness of unapproached being, majesty, glory, as has been described, the immediate and unavoidable conclusion is, that Jesus Christ, by himself and his apostles, claims to be Jehovah; and that as such we must receive him, reverently and joyfully bidding him welcome as one with the Father in the incomprehensible unity of the Godhead; *or else* (forbid the thought, Lord!) we must reject and disown him as the chief adversary of the Divine unity and glory that has ever appeared on the earth.

I cannot but think that all the passages usually cited under the different heads of the *direct* proof of the divinity of Christ, come to acquire a force altogether overwhelming, so soon as the divine Unity has been realized as of that peculiar character which I have attempted to express. Keeping *that* Unity full in view, we bid the Socinian welcome to choose for himself over the entire field of the divine names, perfections, works, worship, whatsoever in Scripture may be considered most peculiar to, and characteristic of, the eternal God. And when he shall have made his choice, we undertake to shew him that which he has chosen ascribed to the Lord Jesus in the Scriptures.

He fixes, let us say, among the divine perfections, on omnipotence. We point him to *Philippians* 3:21, 'The Lord Jesus Christ, who shall change our vile body, that it may be fashioned like unto his glorious body, according to the working whereby he is *able even to subdue all things unto himself.*' He fixes on omniscience. We remind him of *Rev.* 2:23, 'All the churches shall know that I am he which searcheth the reins and hearts.' He fixes on eternity and immutability. We point him to *Heb.* 1:10-12, and *Rev.* 22:13, 'Unto the Son he saith, Thou, Lord, in the beginning hast laid the foundation of the earth; and the heavens are the works of thine hands: they shall perish, but thou remainest; and they all shall wax old as doth a garment; and as a vesture shalt thou fold them up, and they shall be changed: but thou art the same, and thy years shall not fail'; 'I am Alpha and Omega, the beginning and the end, the first and the last.' He fixes on omnipresence. We remind him of those words of Jesus, among many others, *Matt* 18:20, 'Where two or three are gathered together in my name, there am I in the midst of them.' Or, he makes his choice among the most peculiar and characteristic works of God, as creation, 'All things were made by him; and without him was not anything made that was made,' *John* 1:3: preservation of all things, 'Upholding all things by the word of his power,' *Heb.* 1:3: raising the dead, 'I will raise him up at the last day,' *John* 6:40, 44, 54: forgiveness of sins, 'As Christ forgave you, so also do ye,' *Col.*

3:13: saving the soul, 'Jesus who delivered us from the wrath to come;' 'he shall save his people from their sins,' 1 *Thess* 1:10; *Matt* 1:21: judging the world, 'We must all appear before the judgment seat of Christ; that every one may receive the things,' etc.

Or, he prefers to choose among the names and titles of Deity – as, for example, God: 'In the beginning was the Word, and the Word was with God, and the Word was God,' *John* 1:1: the true God, 'We are in him that is true, even in his Son Jesus Christ. This is the true God, and eternal life,' 1 *John* 5:20: I AM, 'Before Abraham was, I am,' *John* 8:58: Jehovah, 'Holy, holy, holy is Jehovah of hosts,' *Isa* 6:3, compared with *John* 12:41, 'These things said Esaias, when he saw his [Christ's] glory, and spake of him:' the mighty God, 'Unto us a child is born: and his name shall be called the mighty God,' *Isa* 9:6: The Alpha and Omega, the first and the last, 'I am Alpha and Omega, the first and the last,' *Rev* 1:11. Or, in fine, he makes his choice from the field of divine worship – prayer: 'Lord Jesus, receive my spirit!' 'The grace of our Lord Jesus Christ be with you all,' *Acts* 7:59; *Rev* 22:21: adoration, thanksgiving, praise, 'Worthy is the Lamb that was slain, to receive power, and riches, and wisdom, and strength, and honour, and glory, and blessing,' *Rev* 5:12.

I have given here but a few specimens of the direct proof under each head, because my object is simply to crave attention to the bearing on that proof, and on the overpowering force of it, of the Scripture doctrine of the divine Unity. Very manifest it is that, if the Lord Jesus be not Jehovah, then so far is the God of the

Bible from being infinitely alone and unapproached in being, excellency, glory, and all perfections, that there is *one creature*, at least, to whom, according to the Scripture, belong absolutely all things whereby God can anywise be distinguished and marked out from his own creatures from all things that are most peculiar to, and characteristic of, the living God – as, indeed, Jesus expressly speaks in *John* 16:15, saying, 'All things that the Father hath are mine.' Socinians speak of Christ's having this thing, and the next thing, *by delegation* from the Father. And it *is* a great and precious truth that he has many things, in the character of Mediator, by delegation from the Father; yea, 'all things,' Jesus said, when speaking in that character, 'are delivered unto me of my Father.' But if it be possible for God to delegate, and if he have actually delegated, to *any mere creature*, all that he himself has – names, perfections, works, worship, glory, with all claims to the supreme affection, homage, love, fear of our innermost hearts – then there is an end at once, and for ever, to the divine Unity, and especially in any such peculiar manner of it as we have seen; and Jesus Christ stands forth *another and second God*, and the chief rival and adversary on earth of the I AM, of the blessed and *only* Potentate, *only* good, *only* holy, *only* wise, who *only* hath immortality, who *only* doeth wondrous things, of whom, and through whom, and to whom, are all things. Perhaps it may help the reader, however, in forming a clearer idea of the bearing of the Scripture doctrine of the divine Unity on the proof of the Saviour's Divinity, if I shall set down, in parallel

[31]

columns, a few examples on either hand, and without distinguishing, in the present instance, between the direct and the incidental – thus:

UNITY OF GOD.	JESUS CHRIST
'I am that I am' (*Exod.* 3:14).	'Before Abraham was, I am' (*John* 8:58).
'Thus saith the Lord the King of Israel, and his redeemer the LORD of hosts; I am the first, and I am the last; and besides me there is no God' *Isa.* 44:6).	'He laid his right hand upon me, saying unto me, Fear not, I am the first and the last' (*Rev.* 1:17).
'Thou only art holy' (*Rev.* 15:4).	'These things saith he that is holy, he that is true' (*Rev.* 3:7).
'There is none good but one, that is God' (*Matt* 19:17).	'That ye may be able to comprehend with all saints, what is the breadth, and length, and depth, and height; and to know the love of Christ, which passeth knowledge' (*Eph* 3:18, 19).
'The only wise God' (1 *Tim* 1:17).	'In whom are hid all the treasures of wisdom and knowledge' (*Col* 2:3).
'The only Potentate' (1 *Tim* 6:15).	'Upholding all things by the word of his power' (*Heb* 1:3).
'Who only hath immortality' (1*Tim* 6:16).	'I am Alpha and Omega, the beginning and the end, the first and the last' (*Rev* 22:13).
'I am the LORD that maketh all things, that stretcheth forth the heavens alone, that spreadeth abroad the earth by myself' (*Isaiah* 44:24).	'All things were made by him; and without him was not anything made that was made' (*John* 1:3).

[32]

'Thou, even thou only, knowest the hearts of all the children of men' (1 *Kings* 8:39).

'All the churches shall know that I am he which searcheth the reins and hearts' (*Rev* 2:23).

'Look unto me, and be ye saved, all the ends of the earth; for I am God, and there is none else' (*Isa* 45:22).

'He shall save his people from their sins' (*Matt* 1:21).

'I kill, and I make alive' (*Deut* 32:39).

'I have the keys of death'; 'I am the resurrection, and the life' (*Rev* 1:18; *John* 11:25).

'Whom have I in heaven but thee? and there is none upon earth that I desire beside thee' (*Ps* 73:25).

'To me to live is Christ'; 'Father, I will that they also whom thou hast given me be with me where I am, that they may behold my glory' (*Phil* 1:21; *John* 17:24).

'My son, give me thine heart' (*Prov* 23:26).

'I have espoused you to one husband, that I may present you as a chaste virgin to Christ' (2 *Cor* 12:2).

'Thou, even thou, art to be feared' (*Ps* 76:7).

'Kiss the Son, lest he be angry, and ye perish from the way when his wrath is kindled but a little'; 'He shall burn the chaff with unquenchable fire'; 'The wrath of the Lamb' (*Ps* 2:12; *Matt* 3:12; *Rev* 6:16).

'Cursed be the man that trusteth in man, and maketh flesh his arm, and whose heart departeth from the LORD' (*Jer* 17:5).

'Kiss the Son. . . . Blessed are all they that put their trust in him'; 'I know whom I have believed, and am persuaded that he is able to keep that which I have committed unto him against that day' (*Ps* 2:12; 2 *Tim* 1:12).

[33]

'Of him, and through him, and to him, are all things; to whom be glory for ever' (*Rom* 11:36).

'All things were created by him, and for him'; 'Christ loved the church, and gave himself for it, . . . that he might present it to himself a glorious church' (*Col* 1:16; *Eph* 5:25, 27).

'Thou shalt worship no other God; for the LORD, whose name is Jealous, is a jealous God' (*Ex* 34:14).

'The grace of our Lord Jesus Christ be with you all'; 'Unto him that loved us, and washed us from our sins in his own blood, and hath made us kings and priests unto God and his Father; to him be glory and dominion for ever and ever. Amen.' (*Rev* 22:21; 1:5, 6).

How entirely evident, that these columns either stand in flat and hopelessly irreconcilable contradiction to each other, or that Jesus Christ, the subject of the second of them, is none other than the God, the Jehovah, of the first. True, indeed, he *also* appears in the second as very man, and the commissioned servant of the Father. But that humanity, and that service (the establishing of which is really the sum and substance of all that Socinians have to allege), are of course quite as much a part of *our* faith, and we glory in finding them quite as clearly and constantly taught in the Scriptures, as the eternal Godhead of the Saviour. Taking the Bible for the only and final standard of our judgment and faith, we believe in the Saviour's Divinity; we believe in his true and very manhood; we believe in the union of the two natures in his one Person; we believe in his mediatorial office and service, as just so many great, palpably revealed, and distinct, though intimately and vitally connected, facts. We accept what Scripture plainly teaches concerning the divine Unity, though quite unable to tell *the manner* of that Unity; unable to tell *the manner* of the harmonizing of it with an everlasting distinction of Persons in the one Godhead; unable to tell *the manner* of the union between the divine and human natures in the Person of the Son; *how*, for us men, and for our salvation, He could become bone of our very bone, and flesh of our very flesh.

Returning, however, to our more proper field of indirect or incidental testimonies to the Divine glory of Christ, and only asking the reader to carry along with him what we have found in this chapter respecting the divine Unity, I take up, in the next one, *the invitations of the Saviour's grace*.

CHAPTER 3

INDIRECT TESTIMONIES OF SCRIPTURE TO THE DIVINE GLORY OF CHRIST FROM THE INVITATIONS OF HIS GRACE.

THE department of incidental testimony to the Saviour's Divinity which occupied us in the opening chapter, was that of *the claims of his authority*. The one to which attention is now briefly called is the *invitations of the Saviour's grace*. I shall select three of them as a specimen of all.

I *John* 7:37, 'In the last day, that great day of the feast, Jesus stood and cried, saying, If any man thirst, let him come unto me, and drink', compared with the words, in the fourth chapter, to the woman of Samaria, 'If thou knewest the gift of God, and who it is that saith to thee, Give me to drink, thou wouldest have asked of him, and he would have given thee living water. . . . Whosoever drinketh of the water that I shall give him shall never thirst; but the water that I shall give him shall be in him a well of water springing up into everlasting life.' *In the last day of the feast, Jesus stood and cried, saying, If any man thirst, let him come unto me, and drink.* I know not how it may strike the reader, after a certain line of thought has been indicated. But I am very sure that the first idea, and by far the most engrossing, if not only one, which is apt to occur to the mind on reading these words, is the *grace* of them, the wondrous unlimited freeness of the Saviour's offer and invitation, 'If any man thirst, let him come unto me, and drink. He that believeth on me, as the scripture hath said, out of his belly shall flow rivers of living water. This spake he of the Spirit, which they that believe on him should receive.' And it is not possible, assuredly, to overestimate the preciousness of this idea, or to fix the mind too earnestly on it. It is the first and leading thought in the passage, and can scarce receive too much attention and regard.

But there lies another thought beneath the surface, not only in itself of unspeakable importance, but lending all possible additional preciousness to the first one. For, let me ask, what manner of man is this, who, in the last day of the feast of tabernacles at Jerusalem, stood, and cried to the vast multitudes who were wont then to assemble in the capital from every quarter, 'If any man thirst, let him come unto me, and drink?' Who is this that bids those multitudes, bids a world, come and draw everlasting refreshment, living water, rivers of living water, the Holy Ghost, from his Person? And, that there may be no possible mistake, as if the reference might perchance have been rather to *instruction where* the living water was to be found, than to the Saviour as himself the giver and source of it, let his words to the Samaritan woman be called to mind, 'Thou wouldest have asked of him, and *he would have given* thee living water.' 'Whosoever drinketh of the water that *I shall give him* shall never thirst.' This, beyond all doubt, 'is the true God, and the eternal life.'

There is a great word of the Old Testament, *'the fountain of living waters'*, occurring there unquestionably as one of the most peculiar and incommunicable titles and characters of Jehovah: 'My people have committed two evils; they have forsaken me, the fountain of living waters, and hewed them out cisterns,' etc. 'They that depart from me shall be written in the earth, because they have forsaken Jehovah, the fountain of living waters' (*Jer* 2:13; 17:13). But behold *that very fountain* here – the very Rock of ages, opened in Jesus Christ, and sending its streams forth for the refreshment of a world, 'Jesus stood and cried, saying, If any man thirst, let him come unto me and drink.' I have often marvelled, in connection with these words, at that one in the record of the crucifixion, 'Jesus, knowing that all things were now accomplished, that the scripture might be fulfilled, saith, I thirst.' Ah, the very fountain of living waters, athirst! And yet this was in reality not more a contrast than an inseparable connection. For what was that thirst, with all the other sufferings of the Lord Jesus, but *the smiting of the rock* (to allude to the type in the wilderness)? What was the whole crucifixion together, but the descending of the Divine lawgiver's rod upon it, the awakening of the sword of the Divine justice 'against the man that was God's fellow,' when he stood charged with our iniquities on this earth, but for which the fountain must have remained, as to us sinners, a spring shut up, a fountain sealed, in Jehovah, Father, Son, and Holy Ghost, for

[39]

ever! And, accordingly, Jesus had no sooner said, 'I thirst,' than another voice was heard from his lips, ' "It is finished:" and he bowed his head, and gave up the ghost.' And 'one of the soldiers with a spear pierced his side, and forthwith came there out blood and water'—

> *' Rock of Ages, cleft for me,*
> *Let me hide myself in thee;*
> *Let the water and the blood,*
> *From thy riven side which flowed,*
> *Be of sin the double cure,*
> *Cleanse me from its guilt and power!'*

'Who is a rock save our God?' (*Ps* 18:31). Who was it, but that very God, that cried in the last day of the feast, and still is crying in the midst of us, 'If any man thirst, let him come unto me, and drink'?

2. *Matt* 11:28, 'Come unto me, all ye that labour and are heavy laden, and I will give you rest.' How gracious! we are ready to exclaim as we listen to these words. How tender, compassionate, loving! And truly they are most gracious words – unutterably loving and compassionate. But *rest – I will give* you rest – a guilty, weary *world* rest? What manner of man is this? Who, save the Almighty God, shall give rest even to one guilty, polluted soul? Ah! others, indeed, may give us this world's riches and treasures, if they happen to possess them, and if they are so inclined. But rest to a sin-laden spirit, rest from the anger of God, rest from

the tyranny of infinite corruptions, rest from our unnumbered burdens and sorrows, what creature shall give us *this*? And not to one soul, nor a myriad of souls, but to a whole world – 'Come unto me, *all* ye that labour and are heavy laden' – sojourn in what country, clime, age soever ye may, be your burdens of what character soever they may! Nor does he say, I will do my best for you; I will give you help in the matter of rest; I will give you directions towards the obtaining of rest; but absolutely, I will *give rest to you*. 'Come unto me, all ye that labour and are heavy laden, and I will give you rest.'

Was ever word like this, or in the remotest degree approaching it, heard from Moses, Elijah, Daniel, Paul, from angel or man? Who *can* this be but the God who said of old time, 'Wherefore do ye spend money for that which is not bread, and your labour for that which satisfieth not? Incline your ear, and *come unto me*; hear, and your soul shall live.' 'Come unto me,' said Jesus Christ, 'and I will give you rest?' Who is this but the God that said, 'Look unto me, and be ye saved, all the ends of the earth; for I am God, and there is none else: surely shall one say, In the LORD have I righteousness and strength; even *to Him shall men come*'; 'Come unto me, and I will give you rest? Who is this but the God of whom David sang, 'Return unto thy rest, O my soul,' and who complained by his servant Jeremiah, 'My people have gone from mountain to hill; they have forgotten their resting place'? 'Come unto me, all ye that labour and are heavy laden, and I will give you rest.'

[41]

True, Jesus does not give this invitation in the *naked character* of God. To speak with deepest reverence, God, simply and nakedly as God, cannot give a sinner rest from his sins – because 'it is impossible for Him to lie;' and 'without the shedding of blood is no remission.' It is in the character of Mediator that our Lord Jesus speaks these great words. And in the previous verse, accordingly, he had said, 'All things are *delivered unto me* of my Father.' But it is well worthy of remark how his Divine glory comes out even there indirectly and incidentally, since no mere creature could, under any character, or for any purpose whatsoever, receive the universe, receive 'all things', from the Father's hand. 'All things are delivered unto me of my Father; and no man knoweth the Son but the Father; neither knoweth any man the Father save the Son, and he to whomsoever the Son will reveal him. Come unto me,' etc.

Before leaving this second testimony, let the reader note how it well exemplifies a remark which was made in the introduction, that, taken up with the grace which lies on the face of such words, we are exceedingly apt to overlook the glory that lies in the heart of them, and thus to lose to a very large extent the very grace wherewith we are too exclusively occupied. Oh the *excellency of the grace* of this invitation, when we have once apprehended and realized the Divine glory of Him who utters it! For mere grace, compassion, can never meet the case of my soul; and majesty alone, apart from infinite compassion, would soon send a soul so guilty into hell. But what a Saviour is this, the fellow of the Lord of hosts, bone also of our bone, and flesh of our flesh, of equal majesty and compassion, power and tenderness, glory and grace: 'All things are delivered unto me of my Father. . . . Come unto me, all ye that labour and are heavy laden, and I will give you rest!'

3. *John* 6:37, 'All that the Father giveth me shall come to me; and *him that cometh to me I will in no wise cast out.*' Let me first ask the reader to note a certain peculiar lustre which marks the *graciousness* of this invitation. The grace of it seems to lie, not simply in the 'him that cometh' – *him*, be he whosoever he may; nor yet merely, in the 'in no wise' – I will on no account whatsoever cast him out. But there is a peculiar character of grace, over and above, in the form of the promise, 'I will not *cast him out.*' For there are states of the soul in which such a negative assurance is found to be even more precious, more easy to be embraced, believed, rested on, than the promise of a crown or a kingdom would be. To a soul weighed down beneath a sense of infinite ill desert, and ready to question the possibility of finding mercy with the Lord at all, there is a singular and manifold graciousness in this whole utterance of Jesus. And accordingly it has been as a very sheet-anchor to many a tempest-tossed child of God in every age. It was this invitation of which the excellent and learned James Durham said on his dying bed, in a time of inward darkness, to the friend who wrote afterwards the memoir of his life, 'After all I have written, and all I have preached, there is but one

word in the Bible I can get any hold of – think you I may venture my soul on it – "him that cometh to me I will in no wise cast out"?' Principal Carstairs replied, 'If you had a hundred souls, you might venture them all on that word.'

Well; but it is just the more necessary, by how much the more gracious the invitation is, that we beware of suffering the grace of it to overshadow *the glory*, the Divine glory of Christ, which shines, as we shall now at once find, in union with the grace, and from which the grace is in fact wholly inseparable. For what creature, let me ask, shall dare to speak of it as a gracious thing at all, that, if his *fellow-creature* come to him, he will not cast him out? What manner of man is this, who, clothed in our nature, indeed, and thus 'not ashamed to call us brethren', yet looks on all men here from a height so immeasurably above them, as to say, If they come to me I will not cast them into hell; if the Emperor of Rome would come to me, I would not reject him; if the Queen of these realms of Britain will come to me, I will not cast her away? Oh, the majesty and the grace are palpably *here* inseparable! The only possible explanation of the grace of such words, imparting also to the graciousness of them an emphasis and an excellency beyond all power of language to express, is found *in the eternal Divinity of him who utters them*, 'All that the Father giveth me shall come to me; and him that cometh to me I will in no wise cast out.'

I cannot close this chapter, however, without recalling to the reader's mind what in the previous one we found, respecting the bearing of the Scripture doctrine of the divine Unity on the proof of the Saviour's Divinity. If, I said, the unity of God were nothing more than some immense superiority over all other beings, then *possibly* such things might be spoken *of* one, or uttered *by* one, who was after all not Jehovah, but only some creature very near to him in the scale of being. But the instant that all such nearness to Him has been discarded as an impossibility, and it has been found that the unity of God, as taught in the Scriptures, imports such a sole, unapproached excellency, glory, in all things, that if you would bring any creature into comparison with him, it is a matter of indifference whether it be an archangel or a worm, the immediate and unavoidable conclusion is, that Jesus Christ claims to be Jehovah, and that as such we must receive him, bidding him welcome as one with the Father in the incomprehensible unity of the Godhead, *or else* must reject and disown him as the chiefest of all adversaries of the divine unity and glory. But no, no! 'Let him kiss me with the kisses of his mouth, for thy love is better than wine!' 'Thou art the king of glory, O Christ; thou art the everlasting Son of the Father. When thou tookest upon thee to deliver man, thou didst not abhor the virgin's womb. When thou hadst overcome the sharpness of death, thou didst open the kingdom of heaven to all believers.' Let the love of this matchless One constrain me to live no more to myself, but to him who died for me, and rose again. Let the invitations of his grace allure and constrain me to bow to the claims of his authority. Hearing his voice, 'Him that cometh to me I will in no wise cast out', 'Come unto me, all ye

[45]

that labour and are heavy laden, and I will give you rest', 'If any man thirst, let him come unto me, and drink,' let me bid welcome also that other voice, 'He that loveth father or mother more than me, is not worthy of me', 'Whether we live, we live unto the Lord; and whether we die, we die unto the Lord; whether we live therefore, or die, we are the Lord's.' '*My love*,' as a martyr of the early Church was wont to speak, 'was crucified.' 'If ye find my Beloved, tell him that I am sick of love.' 'Gird thy sword upon thy thigh, O most Mighty, with thy glory and thy majesty: and in thy majesty ride prosperously, because of truth and meekness and righteousness; and thy right hand shall teach thee terrible things!'

CHAPTER 4

INDIRECT TESTIMONIES TO THE DIVINITY OF CHRIST
FROM COMMENDATIONS OF HIS TRANSCENDENT
EXCELLENCY BY HIMSELF AND HIS SERVANTS, AND
FROM INCIDENTAL REFERENCES TO HIS RANK AND
PLACE AS IN RELATION TO THE FATHER.

COMMENDATIONS of his transcendent excellency *by himself*? How strange this is we fail of perceiving, only because we have grown so familiar with the language of those commendations. For it is a principle witnessed alike by Scripture and by the instincts of our nature, that it is unbecoming in a creature to utter his own praise; that while it is altogether befitting the adorable God to commend his own excellency, the rule for creatures on the contrary is, 'Let another praise thee, and not thine own mouth; a stranger, and not thine own lips' – 'for men to search their own glory, is not glory' (*Prov* 27:2; 25:27). Emphatically, no doubt, the principle applies to *men*, to frail, imperfect men. But it holds also, in reality, of all created and dependent beings, even of the highest angels, who at best can do no more than their duty to God; who thus can never have anything to boast of; and who, fain accordingly to 'cover their faces and their feet with their wings' in His presence, have shrunk back, as often as men, awed by their superior purity and dignity, have bent before them in worship, going no further respecting themselves than that word of one of their number, 'I am Gabriel which stand in the presence of God.'

But now, what manner of man is this whose voice we hear, 'I am the rose of Sharon, and the lily of the valleys', 'I am the bright and morning star', 'I am the good Shepherd', 'I say unto you that in this place is one greater than the temple', 'Behold, a greater than Solomon is here', 'Learn of me, for I am meek and lowly in heart', 'He shall glorify me; for he shall receive of mine, and shall shew it unto you'! I do not take other words, without number, such as, 'I am the first and the last'; 'I am the resurrection and the life'; 'before Abraham was, I am', because these are not mere self-commendations, but direct claims to Divinity, if language have any significance, and do not therefore fall within our field of indirect testimonies. I take simply *the principle of self-commendation*. And here it is well worthy of being noticed that, not only is it not felt to be a thing unbefitting our Lord Jesus to speak his own praise, but, just as the glorious God never appears more glorious than when proclaiming his own excellencies (as to Job, for example, out of the whirlwind), so Christ never seems fairer, or more attractive, than when commending himself, as I remember to have heard of a humble, godly woman, who said of him, 'It *sets him weel* to commend *himsel*.' O yes, Paul was obliged in some of his epistles to speak his own praise. But again and again he apologizes for it, calls it 'speaking as a fool', and declares he had recourse to it only because the Corinthians had compelled him. The Lord Jesus, offering no apology, never seems lovelier in the eyes of his people than when saying, 'I am the good Shepherd', 'I am the rose of Sharon', 'I am meek and lowly in heart', 'I am the root and the offspring of David, and the bright and morning star'. The fitting response on our part, what is it but Thomas's, 'My Lord and my God'? But let us now, a little more fully, look at some commendations of the Saviour's transcendent excellency *by his servants*. I select John the Baptist, the Gentile centurion of Capernaum, and the apostle Paul.

First, the forerunner of Christ: *Luke* 3:16, 17, 'John answered saying unto them all, I indeed baptize you with water; but one mightier than I cometh, the latchet of whose shoes I am not worthy to unloose; he shall baptize you with the Holy Ghost and with fire: whose fan is in his hand, and he will thoroughly purge his floor, and will gather the wheat into his garner; but the chaff he will burn with fire unquenchable.' *One mightier than I cometh, the latchet of whose shoes I am not worthy to unloose,* or, as Mark has it, *to stoop down and unloose.* Ah! who is this for whom the stern and unbending John, that would not have quailed before the mightiest potentate on earth, counted himself unworthy to do even the office of a slave? It is the practice, it seems, in China, for persons brought before the higher authorities on a criminal charge, to kneel before them on both knees. A few years ago, a devoted Scottish Missionary was charged with an offence connected with his great work, and, on being summoned before one of those authorities, was ordered to kneel in the usual manner. 'I am willing,' he replied, 'to kneel, if you desire it, on one knee, as I would before the sovereign of England. But I cannot go down on both knees before any but Jehovah.' Oh, I think John the Baptist is bending lower than on both knees before Christ in these words, 'One mightier than I cometh, the latchet of whose shoes I am not worthy to stoop down and unloose.'

But the testimony, the commendation, is not done: 'Whose fan is in his hands, and he will thoroughly purge his floor' – *his* floor – so that the whole visible Church on earth is the property of Jesus Christ, '*his* floor'. 'And he will gather the wheat into his garner.' All heaven too, it seems, is his property – 'he will gather the wheat into *his* garner; but the chaff *he will burn* with fire unquenchable.' Hell also, it seems, is his, kindled by his breath – '*He* will burn the chaff.' Compare those words, 2 *Thess* 1:7, 8, 'When the Lord Jesus shall be revealed from heaven with his mighty angels, in flaming fire *taking vengeance* on them that know not God, and obey not the gospel of our Lord Jesus Christ.' 'The chaff he will burn with fire unquenchable.' O Lamb of God that takest away the sin of the world, let thy precious blood be ever upon my poor soul; and baptize thou me with the Holy Ghost, that 'fire' which consumes only the sin, but melts and refines and purifies the sinner!

Second, the Gentile centurion of Capernaum: *Luke* 7:6-8, 'Then Jesus went with them. And when he was now not far from the house, the centurion sent friends to him, saying unto him, Lord, trouble not thyself; for

I am not worthy that thou shouldest enter under my roof; wherefore neither thought I myself worthy to come unto thee; but say in a word, and my servant shall be healed. For I also am a man set under authority, having under me soldiers: and I say unto one, Go, and he goeth; and to another, Come, and he cometh; and to my servant, Do this, and he doeth it.' See, first, how this believing soldier ascribes to Jesus so transcendent a purity and glory, that neither is he himself worthy so much as to approach him, nor worthy that Jesus should approach at all to *him* – 'Lord, trouble not thyself, for I am not worthy that thou shouldest enter under my roof; wherefore neither thought I myself worthy to come unto thee.' And further, behold how he ascribes to him such a resistless, unlimited authority and power, that with the same ease wherewith *he* could say to one of his soldiers, Go, and he should go, with the very same ease Jesus had but to speak to death, to disease, to all nature, and it should obey him – 'say in a word, and my servant shall be healed: for I also am a man set under authority, having under me soldiers; and I say unto one, Go, and he goeth'. He does not even think it necessary to draw the conclusion in as many words, The like absolute authority, Lord, hast thou over death, disease, all things whatsoever. He silently assumes, takes it for granted.

But Jesus perhaps will shrink back from such a commendation, in the spirit of that angel who, when the apostle John in an unguarded moment fell at his feet, said, 'See thou do it not, for I am thy fellow-servant, and of thy brethren the prophets, and of them

which keep the sayings of this book; worship God'?
Nay, for it is written in the next verse, 'When Jesus
heard these things, he marvelled at him, and turned
him about, and said unto the people that followed him,
I say unto you, I have not found *so great faith*, no, not
in Israel.' Thus He whom we just now found uttering
his own praise, and offering no kind of apology for it,
bids welcome the praise of the centurion as nothing
more than his due, 'I have not found so great faith, no,
not in Israel.' With which compare, in passing, the
Syrophenician woman's words, 'Lord, help me. But
he said, It is not meet to take the children's bread, and
to cast it to dogs. And she said, Truth, Lord; yet the
dogs eat of the crumbs which fall from their master's
table' – I, the dog; thou, the master! 'Jesus answered
and said unto her, O woman, *great is thy faith*; be it
unto thee even as thou wilt.' It is, and can be, none
other than the God to whom the prophet of old
addressed himself, 'Heal me, O Jehovah, and I shall
be healed; save me, and I shall be saved: for thou art
my praise.'

Third, the apostle Paul. I take two examples from
his Epistles. First, his remarkable words addressed to
the Corinthians (1 *Cor* 2:2), 'I determined not to know
anything among you, save Jesus Christ, and him
crucified.' *Not to know anything among them save Jesus
Christ?* Behold an inspired teacher of religion, passing
from city to city, from church to church, determined
to know but one thing, as it were; teach but one thing;
publish, commend, enforce, glory in one thing – a
creature? O frightful thought, and contradiction in the

very terms! For religion is but another word for God. God is religion; religion is God. When this inspired teacher, therefore, determines not to know anything in the churches save Jesus Christ, he evidently assumes and presupposes that Christ is God – God the Son, who, for us men, and for our salvation, became flesh, and therein died, the Just for the unjust. 'I determined not to know any among you save Jesus Christ, and him crucified.'

Then, a second example of Paul's commendations of the transcendent excellency and beauty of the Lord Jesus: *Eph* 3:17–19, 'That Christ may dwell in your hearts by faith; that ye, being rooted and grounded in love, may be able to comprehend with all saints, what is the breadth, and length, and depth, and height; and to know the love of Christ, which passeth knowledge.' *The breadth, and length, and depth, and height of the love of Christ, which passeth knowledge.* It is enough simply to say here, that no higher commendation *can* be pronounced, or conceived, of the love of the eternal God. The inspired apostle here exhausts all the powers of language in the praise of the love *of Christ*, so that, were He not very and eternal God, there could remain no higher possible praise for the Divine love to receive – 'the breadth, and length, and depth, and height of the love of Christ, which passeth knowledge'. If anything could add to the force of this indirect testimony to the Divinity of the Lord Jesus, it would be those words of the Saviour himself (unless, indeed, he and his apostle flatly contradict each other!), 'there is none good but one, that is God'; of course teaching that so entirely alone, and unapproached in excellency, is the goodness and love of Jehovah, that all the love, the goodness, even of *the highest and noblest creatures in the universe*, brought into comparison with it, are extinguished as some taper-light in the sun, and are as if they had no existence. 'There is none good but one, that is God.' 'That ye may be able to comprehend with all saints what is the breadth, and length, and depth, and height; and to know *the love of Christ*, which passeth knowledge, that ye might be filled with all the fulness of God.'

But I have noted, in the title of this chapter, one other class of indirect testimonies to the Divine glory of Christ – *incidental Scripture references to his rank and place as in relation to the Father.*

1. In the fourteenth chapter of John's Gospel, there will be found a whole cluster of such references. Take ver. 23, 'Jesus answered and said unto him, If a man love me, he will keep my words; and my Father will love him, and we will come unto him, and make our abode with him.' *We, the Father and I*, Jesus says, will come unto him, and make *our* abode with him. Palpably he places himself there on a level with the eternal Father – 'we'! Some madman perhaps would say of the sovereign of this country. 'The Queen and I' – *we* will do this or that. Of him before whom all sovereigns, yea, all creatures in the universe, are less than nothing, and vanity, Jesus says, 'we' – 'my Father will love him, and *we* will come unto him, and make out abode with him'.

Or compare the words of an earlier chapter. 'Therefore did the Jews persecute Jesus, and sought to slay him, because he had done these things on the Sabbathday. But Jesus answered them, My Father worketh hitherto, *and I work*'; or those words, 'It is written in your law that the testimony of two men is true. I am one that bear witness of myself, *and* the Father that sent me beareth witness of me.' 'We will come unto him, and make our abode with him': a fine example, by the way, of that quiet taking for granted of Christ's Divinity, in the Scriptures, of which I have repeatedly spoken; how, instead of its being taught only in some great and special places, it runs as a golden thread gloriously through the whole.

Or take ver. 13 and 14, 'Whatsoever ye shall ask in my name, that will I do, that the Father may be glorified in the Son. If ye shall ask anything in my name, I will do it.' Here, with the like quiet majesty Jesus assumes (I say *assumes*, although it is an express declaration, because the thing more properly and formally declared and affirmed is the certainty in general of a gracious answer to prayer offered in the name of the Son; but he further assumes and declares, as it were in passing) this stupendous fact, that all and whatsoever things believers receive in answer to their prayers, are done for them, bestowed on them, by him, the Lord Jesus Christ – 'whatsoever ye shall ask in my name, *that will I do*; if ye shall ask anything in my name, *I will do it*.' Or take ver. 7–9, 'If ye had known me, ye should have known my Father also; and from henceforth ye know him, and have seen him. Philip saith unto him, Lord, shew us the Father, and it sufficeth us. Jesus saith unto him, Have I been so long time with you, and yet hast thou not known me, Philip? He that hath seen me hath seen the Father; and how sayest thou then, Shew us the Father?' Only let the reader glance back on the thoughts of the second chapter regarding the Unity of God, that infinite chasm which subsists between Jehovah and all creatures, the greatest and highest; and then let him read, 'Lord, shew us the Father, and it sufficeth us. Have I been so long time with you, and yet hast thou not known *me*, Philip? He that hath seen me hath seen the Father, and how sayest thou then, Shew us the Father?'

Or, yet again in this chapter, ver. 28, 'Ye have heard how I said unto you, I go away, and come again unto you. If ye loved me, ye would rejoice, because I said, I go unto the Father; for my Father is greater than I.' The testimony is in these last words, 'My Father is greater than I.' For it is very easy to see, no doubt, how it should have been necessary for the Lord to remind the disciples, after all those previous claims to essential equality and oneness with the Father, that there was a very important respect in which the Father was greater than he, even his humanity, and whole mediatorial character and office. But, assuredly, *save for* such a presupposed, essential and everlasting, oneness and equality, on supposition that Jesus never had been anything more than a creature, and servant of the Father, it had been nothing else than blasphemous trifling with all sacred things, to tell the disciples coolly, that the adorable God was 'greater than he'! O, well might they in such a case have demanded, like their countrymen before, 'Whom makest thou thyself?' 'My Father is greater than I!'*

* Since the above was written, I have observed the following very comprehensive 'Remarks', subjoined to my beloved brother Dr David Brown's Exposition of this chapter, in his invaluable Work, 'Critical, Experimental and Practical Commentary on the New Testament':

'Look at the varied lights in which Jesus holds forth *Himself* to the confidence and love and obedience of His disciples. To their fluttering hearts – ready to sink at the prospect of His sufferings, His departure from them, and their own desolation without Him, to say nothing of His cause when left in such incompetent hands – His opening words are, "Let not your heart be troubled: ye believe in God, believe also in Me." "Though clouds and darkness are round about Him, and His judgments are a great deep, yet *ye believe in God*. What time, then, your heart is overwhelmed, *believe in Me*, and darkness shall become light before you, and crooked things straight." What a claim is this on the part of Jesus – to be in the Kingdom of Grace precisely as God is in that of Nature and Providence, or rather to be the glorious Divine Administrator of all things whatsoever in the interests and for the purposes of Grace; in the shadow of Whose wings, therefore, all who believe in God are to put their implicit trust, for the purposes of salvation! For He is not sent merely to *show* men the way to the Father, no, nor merely to *prepare* that way; but Himself *is* the Way, and the Truth, and the Life. We go not *from* Him, but *in* Him, to the Father. For He is in the Father, and the Father in Him; the words that He spake are the Father's words, and the works that He did are the Father's works; and he that hath seen Him hath seen the Father, for he is the Incarnate manifestation of the Godhead. But there are other views of Himself, equally transcendent, in which Jesus holds himself forth here. To what a cheerless distance did He seem to be going away, and when and where should His disciples ever find him again? " 'Tis but to my Father's home," He replies, "and in due time it is to be yours too." In that home there will not only be

2. Leaving this noble chapter, let me, secondly, among incidental references to the Saviour's rank and place, invite attention to *John* 11:4, 'When Jesus heard that, he said, This sickness is not unto death, but for the glory of God, that the Son of God might be glorified thereby.' Here, if I mistake not, there are *two* great

---

room for all, but a mansion for each. But it is not ready yet, and He is going to prepare it for them. For them He is going thither; for them He is to live there; and, when the last preparations are made, for them He will at length return, to take them to that home of His Father, and their Father, that *where He is, there they may be also*. The attraction of heaven to those who love Him is, it seems, to be His Own presence there, and the beatific consciousness that they are *where He is* – language intolerable in a *creature*, but in Him who is the Incarnate, manifested Godhead, supremely worthy, and to his believing people in every age unspeakably re-assuring. But again, He had said that in heaven He was to occupy himself in preparing a place for them; so, a little afterwards, He tells them one of the ways in which this was to be done. To "hear prayer" is the exclusive prerogative of Jehovah, and one of the brightest jewels in His crown. But, says Jesus here, "Whatsoever ye shall ask of the Father in My name, THAT WILL I DO" – not as interfering with, or robbing God of His glory, but on the contrary – "that the Father may be glorified in the Son: If ye shall ask anything in My name, I WILL DO IT." Further, He is the *Life* and the *Law* of His people. Much do we owe to Moses; much to Paul; but never did either say to those who looked up to them, "Because I live, ye shall live also; if ye love Me, keep My commandments; If a man love Me, he will keep My words, and my Father will love him, and WE will come unto him, and make OUR abode with him." '

Among many other important features of this Work, I know of no Commentary on the Gospels comparable with it in respect of the light which it everywhere casts on the peculiar theme of the present little volume.

and distinct testimonies to the Divinity of the Lord Jesus. For, first, it is a fundamental principle of Scripture, that all things are for the *glory* of God alone; many ways for the benefit of the creature, but for the glory, not of the creature, but only of him 'of whom, and through whom, and *to* whom are all things.' I go into no proof of this, but assume it as beyond question. Well; but if Jesus were not the eternal God, then does he simply mount here into his place and throne, trampling that grand principle in the dust. 'This sickness,' says he, 'is not unto death, but for the glory of God, *that the Son of God might be glorified thereby.*' Compare those words of a previous chapter, 'This beginning of miracles did Jesus in Cana of Galilee, and *manifested forth his glory*'; or those words of an after one, respecting the office of the Holy Ghost, 'He shall *glorify me*; for he shall receive of mine, and shall shew it unto you'; or those of Paul in second Thessalonians, 'When he shall come *to be glorified* in his saints, and *admired* in all them that believe.' 'This sickness is not unto death, but for the glory of God, that the Son of God might be glorified thereby.' But then, besides, be it observed how our Lord here quietly interchanges 'God', and 'the Son of God', – interchanges them as all one substantially, differing only in some particular respects. 'This sickness,' he says, 'is not unto death, but for the glory of God, that the Son of God might be glorified thereby,' as if he had said, 'for the glory of God,' and *more specifically and immediately*, 'that the Son of God might be glorified thereby.'

3. This last form of the double testimony in those words, which I have called the quiet interchanging of 'God', and 'the Son of God', runs into a whole series of examples of a like interchange, with a very few of which I bring to a close our indirect or incidental testimonies to the Divine glory of Christ. Thus, *Rom* 8:35, 38, 39, 'Who shall separate us from the *love of Christ*? Shall tribulation, or distress, or persecution, or famine, or nakedness, or peril, or sword? . . . I am persuaded that neither death, nor life, nor angels, nor principalities, nor powers, nor things present, nor things to come, nor height, nor depth, nor any other creature, shall be able to separate us from the *love of God*, which is in Christ Jesus our Lord.' It will at once be perceived that 'the love *of Christ*' in the opening verse, and 'the love *of God*' in the closing one, are used by the apostle as interchangeable terms, having substantially the same meaning. 'Who shall separate us from the love *of Christ?*' is the question asked. The answer to it is, Nothing 'shall be able to separate us from the love *of God* which is in Christ Jesus our Lord'. Again, the ninth verse of the same chapter, 'Ye are not in the flesh, but in the Spirit, if so be that the Spirit of God dwell in you. Now if any man have not the Spirit of Christ, he is none of his.' The Spirit *of God* and the Spirit *of Christ* are interchanged as being all one substantially. Or, *Rom* 14:10–12, 'But why dost thou judge thy brother? or why dost thou set at nought thy brother? for we shall all stand before the judgment-seat *of Christ*. For it is written, As I live, saith the Lord, every knee shall bow to me, and every

tongue shall confess *to God*. So then every one of us shall give account of himself to God.' To bow before Christ, to bow before God, the judgment-seat of Christ, the judgment-seat of God, these are one. The terms are familiarly interchanged. One other instance, which requires no comment. *Eph* 6:5-9, 'Servants, be obedient to them that are your masters according to the flesh, with fear and trembling, in singleness of your heart, *as unto Christ*; not with eye-service, as men pleasers; but as the servants of Christ, doing *the will of God* from the heart; with good will doing service, as to the Lord, and not to men; knowing that whatsoever good thing any man doeth, the same shall he receive of the Lord, whether he be bond or free. And ye masters, do the same things to them, forbearing threatening: knowing that your *Master* also is in heaven; neither is there respect of persons with him.'

But now it will be found that a wide field of *inference*, alike doctrinal and practical, opens to us on a review of all that has come before us in the previous pages. In a fifth chapter, I mean to notice *the bearings of the whole on some fatal forms of doctrinal error*, and, in a sixth, *its bearings on Christian faith and life*.

CHAPTER 5

BEARINGS OF THE WHOLE ON SOME FATAL FORMS OF DOCTRINAL ERROR.

1. FIRST, Infidelity. Out of those indirect or incidental testimonies to the Divinity of Christ which we have found scattered up and down over his recorded words and discourses, there comes, I am persuaded, a collateral argument of very great interest and weight against infidelity, for the certain truth of our Lord's mission and gospel. For, let the state of the case be observed. There lived once on earth a man who claimed to be a teacher sent from God, whose claim, however, in the form and manner and import of it, was in the last degree extraordinary and unparalleled. Confessed, on all hands, to have asserted and vindicated the glory of the one true and living God as none had ever done before him, he yet claimed, as we have found, to be not the *servant* of that God only, but his *equal* also, essentially and eternally; not only sent and commissioned by him, in one respect and character, but *one* with him in another and higher; one in nature, in glory, and in all perfections. From the same lips which are acknowledged by all to have revealed and asserted the glory of Jehovah as none had done before, came words, habitually, which could mean nothing short of

a claimed equality with the Father: 'If a man love me, he will keep my words; and my Father will love him, and *we* will come unto him, and make our abode with him'; 'Come unto me, all ye that labour and are heavy laden, and *I will give you rest*'; 'Have I been so long time with you, and yet hast thou not known me, Philip? he that hath seen me hath seen the Father, and how sayest thou then, Shew us the Father?'; 'I am the resurrection, and the life'; 'Depart from *me*, ye cursed, into everlasting fire,' etc., etc. And then, besides such altogether unparalleled claims, be it remembered that, as man, Jesus claimed to be *entirely without sin*; compassed, indeed, with manifold sinless infirmities common to him with our race, but amidst them all stainless; without a taint of defilement in nature, thought, speech, action.

How *could* such extraordinary claims, at once to Divinity, and to an absolutely sinless humanity, have been by possibility put forth, without the speedy and unavoidable detection of their folly and falsehood, *if they were false indeed*, if they were either the arts of an impostor, or the dreams of an enthusiast and fanatic? For it was no hermit life that Jesus led, coming forth only for an occasional hour to the public view, and then hastening back into seclusion. 'I spake openly to the world,' he said on the morning of his crucifixion day; 'I ever taught in the synagogue, and in the temple, whither the Jews always resort; and in secret have I said nothing. Why askest thou me? ask them which heard me, what I have said unto them: behold, they know what I said.' And *for three successive years* Jesus taught thus among his countrymen. He put forth these extraordinary claims during that long period, alike among skilful and malignant enemies who watched for his halting, and among familiar friends, who, with constant opportunities of witnessing incongruities, if there were any, in his language and life, had no possible inducements to cling to his service, save those arising out of a profound conviction of the truth of his claims.

Behold him, for example, accepting Simon the Pharisee's invitation to eat with him, with all possible calmness and self-possession asserting those claims at his table, meeting his fancied triumph, 'This man, if he were a prophet, would have known who and what manner of woman this is that toucheth him, for she is a sinner,' in the parable of the two debtors, which we found to have been nothing short of a claim to be himself the glorious, Divine creditor, to whom the debt of all Simon's sins, and of the woman's alike, was owing.

And so, the gospel histories are full of scenes of our Lord's teaching like the following: 'He entered into the synagogue, and there was a man there which had a withered hand. And they watched him whether he would heal on the Sabbath day, that they might accuse him'; 'It came to pass, as he went into the house of one of the chief Pharisees, to eat bread on the Sabbath day, that they watched him'; 'As he said these things unto them, the scribes and the Pharisees began to urge him vehemently, and to provoke him to speak of many things; laying wait for him, and seeking to catch something out of his mouth, that they might accuse him.'

Or think, on the other hand, of the same exalted claims put forth amid the quiet intercourse of the sojournings with the family of Bethany, or in the intimacy of the daily and uninterrupted converse with the twelve. How unavoidable was it that the madness of them, *if they were indeed false*, should have come out over and over again, among enemies and friends alike! How certain that, neither as a deceiver, nor as a fanatic, Jesus could have spoken and acted in any decent consistency with such claims, for six months, not to speak of three years! Even supposing a deceiver to have been capable of forming the idea of a mission and work of such unequalled greatness as that of our Lord Jesus, he never could have *spoken and acted the part*, with any appearance of truth. And assuredly, he would have taken excellent care to shun all those acts of lowly and frank and condescending familiarity, of which the life of Jesus is so full, lest, in the freedom of them, he should let the mask drop off, and miss the reverence and awe with which he wished to be regarded. But Jesus, issuing forth from the obscurest condition, lays claim to quite unheard-of dignities, puts himself on a level with God, proclaims himself the Searcher of hearts, the Resurrection and the Life, the Saviour and Judge of the world, and enters, at the same time, without any restraint, into all kinds of circumstances and situations, in no single instance speaking or acting beneath his unparalleled character and claims!

He speaks of performing the most Divine actions,

such as saving the world, bestowing everlasting life, raising the dead, with the same ease and familiarity wherewith we speak of doing the commonest things. 'Our friend Lazarus sleepeth,' he said; 'but I go that I may awake him out of sleep.' It was his manner of intimating his intention to raise Lazarus out of his grave, 'I go that I may awake him out of sleep'; as easy, it seems, for him to raise the dead, as for us to touch a friend in the morning, and awake him! And the disciples accordingly failing to apprehend his meaning, said, ' "Lord, if he sleep, he shall do well." Howbeit Jesus spake of his death; but they thought that he had spoken of taking of rest in sleep. Then said Jesus unto them plainly, Lazarus is dead; and I am glad for your sakes that I was not there, to the intent ye may believe; nevertheless let us go unto him' – *go to the dead man* – to Lazarus, four days buried in his grave! Such claims, so asserted, are self-proving, self-demonstrative.

'Suffer the little children to come unto me,' said he, 'and forbid them not, for of such is the kingdom of God. And he took them up in his arms, put his hands upon them, and blessed them.' Behold the heart of Jesus there, ineffably tender, gracious, gentle; the entire reverse of everything harsh, selfish, proud, unloving. Ay, but he had just before been giving forth laws respecting the marriage relation, that were destined soon to change the face of the world, and are, in fact, moulding the whole civilized world at this hour. (See the previous verses, *Mark* 10:2-12.) And the disciples, accordingly, overawed by the greatness of their Master, and incapable of realizing a tenderness and gentleness quite as great in union with it, ventured to think *for him*, that it was enough he should have given laws for families and parents, without being asked to concern himself with their infants, incapable of profiting by his instructions. But behold the Master with infinite ease passing from the majesty of a universal lawgiver to the tenderness of a very nursing mother, 'Suffer the little children to come unto me, and forbid them not. And he took them up in his arms, put his hands upon them, and blessed them.' Oh, it is he who shortly before had arisen in that vessel, and rebuked the wind, and said to the sea, 'Peace be still; and there was a great calm.' 'He took up the little children in his arms, put his hands upon them, and blessed them!' It is he whose face, on the mount of transfiguration, did shine as the sun, and his raiment was white as the light; and there came a voice to him from the excellent glory, 'This is my beloved Son, in whom I am well pleased.' And, when the three disciples, overpowered by the whole scene, fell on their faces, sore afraid, Jesus, no wise moved or elated, as if nothing strange had happened, 'came and touched them, and said, Arise, and be not afraid.' *Now*, he takes up the little children in his arms, puts his hands upon them, and blesses them! It is he from whose lips came the words, 'The hour is coming in which all that are in the graves shall hear the voice of the Son of man, and shall come forth'; 'Suffer the little children to come unto me, and forbid them not. And he took them up in his arms, put his hands upon them, and blessed

[68]

them!' I repeat that such a character and history are self-proving. No impostor could have lived the character, or could have attempted to live it, without discovering the artifice at every step. No false historian could have *conceived* the character, to fabricate and write it.

I remember having been struck, more than twenty years ago, with an argument for the truth of our Lord's mission, in the Essays of Channing, the well-known Socinian writer of America – so far drawn from the materials of proof I am now dealing with – from the utter impossibility, save on supposition of the truth of his claims, of Christ's having combined in his character and teaching and life, such elements of grandeur and lowliness, majesty and meekness, greatness and tenderness – and this, without the slightest appearance of constraint or effort, among enemies and friends alike, and under every possible variety of circumstances. But, in the first place, I think it were not difficult to shew that, on the Socinian hypothesis of a mere highly gifted man, the greatness, the majesty, the grandeur, had been altogether out of place; would have been nothing else than arrogance and blasphemy. And, second, it *is* no doubt true – apart from questions regarding the constitution of the Saviour's person – that the combination of those divers elements, in so perfect a harmony, in his character and life, demonstrates the truth of his mission. But, in the third place, the argument is then only to be seen in its full and overwhelming force, when the claimed greatness and grandeur are beheld as none other than the grandeur and greatness of everlasting Godhead! Oh, *then* does it become entirely evident that no one falsely asserting such claims, whether as a half-insane enthusiast, or as a cunning deceiver, could have avoided ten thousand incongruities and inconsistencies, exposing his wild pretensions, equally to the scorn of enemies, and to the detection of those familiar friends, who, as I have said, had no possible inducement to choose his service, apart from an unalterable conviction of *the truth* of his claims, and of all the peculiar promises which were dependent on them.

2. Second, Arianism. To one desirous of escaping from the mystery of the Trinity, one who looks at that mystery from certain limited points of view, and is, at the same time, loath to go quite so far down as the Socinian theory of a mere man, it is apt to seem as if some escape might be found from the difficulties, in the Arian hypothesis of a superangelic Being, more or less approaching, though not actually of, the rank and nature of the true and living God. But what comes of that whole hypothesis, in connection with what we have found to be the Scripture doctrine of the Divine *unity*, consigning the entire idea of such an approach to God on the part even of the highest and noblest of creatures, to the place of an impossibility and a blasphemy? In other respects, indeed, the Arian hypothesis (besides the endless difficulties common to it with the Socinian theory) has distinct difficulties of its own, at least as great as those which beset the latter; inasmuch as the evidence of a true and proper *humanity*

stands so palpably out on every page of the Gospels. Still, there have always been minds – some of them of a high order – which, equally averse from acknowledging the proper Divinity of Christ, on the one hand, and resting in his mere humanity, on the other, have been inclined to take refuge in a middle ground, in the Arian theory of a highly exalted Being, neither God, nor man, but of some intermediate, superangelic rank, such as perchance might explain the higher and diviner things ascribed to Jesus in the Scriptures. I believe that the whole idea springs, however, and derives all the plausibility it has, simply from low thoughts of Jehovah's infinite, unapproached, and unapproachable excellency and glory.

And here I am anxious to refer back, for a moment, to an extract which was made in the second chapter, that on the bearing of the Scripture doctrine of the Divine Unity on the proof of the Divinity of Christ, from an author whose name I then preferred not to mention, describing him as an illustrious writer of the 18th century. Let me now state that the writer was Dr Samuel Clarke, who, though a Rector of the Church of England, was believed to hold Arian, or semi-Arian, opinions. The passage occurs in a series of Discourses on the Attributes of God (not the famous volume of the Boyle Lecture), and has reference to the title in Exodus, 'I AM,' along with that one in the Apocalypse, 'Him which is, and which was, and which is to come.' I will again quote the passage: 'Other things also are, and have been, and shall be. But because what they have been, might have been otherwise; and what they

are, might as possibly not have been at all; and what
they shall be, may be very different from what now is:
therefore of their changeable and dependent essence,
which to-day may be one thing, and to-morrow another
thing, and the next day possibly nothing at all; of such
a dependent and changeable essence, compared with
the invariable existence of God, it scarce deserves to be
affirmed that it *is*.' Now I am no wise concerned to
reconcile this learned man *with himself*. But I am very
sure of this, that the doctrine of the above passage
must be recalled and renounced, before the Arian
theory, in any form or grade of it, higher or lower, can
even *seem* for a moment to be reconcilable with the
Holy Scriptures; that, for this purpose, it must be
held, in opposition to the whole doctrine of the passage,
that there is *one* creature at least, who, in place of being
separated by so vast a distance from the 'I AM', that it
scarce deserves to be affirmed of him that he *is*, is, on
the contrary, clothed in Scripture so universally with
the names, titles, perfections, works, worship, of
Jehovah, that it is impossible to fix on any one thing,
no matter how distinctively characteristic of him,
which is not ascribed to this creature in the inspired
volume! Assuredly, however, Dr Clarke does nothing
more than justice to those titles of God he is comment-
ing on. And we have found how thoroughly the
comment is in harmony with the teaching of Scripture
respecting the Divine unity; not as to being or essence
only, but perfections also, works, glory, worship; how,
in respect of them all, the I AM, the blessed and only
Potentate, only good, only holy, is separated by a

chasm so vast from all creatures, even the noblest and highest, that if any of them shall be brought into comparison with him, it signifies nothing how low the compared creature is, or how high, 'the LORD, the LORD God' standing quite alone in respect of all alike. It follows of course, that the Arian hypothesis can, just as little as the Socinian, afford relief from the only alternative which is left, namely, that the Lord Jesus Christ either is Jehovah, one with the Father in the incomprehensible unity of the Godhead, or else is the rival of Jehovah – by far the most formidable rival and adversary of the Divine unity and glory that ever appeared on the earth.

3. Third, Romanism. It may perhaps to some occur to ask, what bearing, at least of any special kind, our theme of Christ's Divine glory can have on Romanism, since the Church of Rome has ever been zealous for the doctrines of the Trinity, and the Divinity of the Saviour. And so it *has* been, no doubt, in some sense – as regards *the letter* of these doctrines. But meanwhile, alas! the whole idea of Divinity, as presented in the sacred volume, the whole Scriptural idea of the glory of the one true and living God, has in Romanism been in effect vitiated and lost. Let but the unity of God be still viewed as importing, not some mere immense superiority over all other beings, but such an aloneness of unapproached and unapproachable glory, in nature and in all perfections, as in these pages we have seen; let that infinite chasm be but realized, which we have found dividing the one living God from all creatures in

the universe; let the Divine unity be seen as it comes out in all words of Scripture like these: 'I am, and there is none beside me'; 'Thou only art holy'; 'The blessed and only Potentate'; 'There is one lawgiver, who is able to save and to destroy'; 'Him with whom we have to do'; 'There is none good but one, that is God'; 'Thou, even thou only, knowest the hearts of all the children of men'; 'I will not give my glory to another'; 'Thou shalt worship no other God; for Jehovah, whose name is Jealous, is a jealous God' – then, immediately, Rome's whole vast fabric of crea- ture-worship stands out, a mass of baptized *polytheism!*

In vain, to escape from that charge, she repeats and chants her 'Credo in unum Deum'. Innumerable creatures are the while invested by her, in different measures and degrees, with God's inalienable func- tions, attributes, actions, worship. In vain Rome, like the Socinian, deals in different kinds of religious worship, and speaks of delegated functions and powers. The polytheism of *heathen* Rome never excluded, nor does that of Hindostan at this day exclude, one *supreme* Deity, raised far above the other objects of worship. When the angel refused the worship which John was about to offer to him, and Peter refused that of Cornelius, it was doubtless an inferior worship which was offered in both cases. *At the head* of Rome's hierarchy of worshipped Beings Jehovah stands, no doubt. But next to Him, 'the Queen of Angels', and 'Mistress of the World', is receiving the highest species of creature-worship; and next come the angels and saints, receiving a worship somewhat lower. And even on earth, what else than a worshipped demigod is 'the most holy Father' at Rome, dispensing with oaths and Divine laws, unlocking the treasures of the Divine mercy to sinners, telling the years by which he, 'the good Father', is pleased to shorten the torment of souls in the unseen world, and receiving the tiara, (as the Roman Pontiffs all do at their coronation,) in these shocking words – 'Receive the tiara, adorned with the triple crown, and know that thou art the Father of princes and of kings, the Ruler of the world upon earth, the Vicar of our Saviour Jesus Christ.'

I think Pope Clement VII. and his cardinals did no more than throw the thin disguise off for a moment when they said once, in a letter to Charles V., 'As there is only one God in heaven, so there cannot, and there ought not to be, but one God on earth!' Especially, however, it is in the *heaven* of the Church of Rome that her polytheism is seen in its chief nakedness: for that heaven is as full of gods and goddesses as there are in it canonized saints, to share thus frightfully with the Father and the Son the homage and affection of the Church. I quote a prayer found in the forefront of each of the four volumes of the Roman Breviary, the prayer-book of the Romish priesthood; prepared in virtue of a decree of the Council of Trent; sanctioned by Popes Pius V., Clement VIII., and Urban VIII.; and of which all Romish ecclesiastics are to this day bound to repeat daily a lesson or office, on pain of mortal sin—

'To the most holy and undivided Trinity, to the humanity of our crucified Lord Jesus Christ, to the fruitful integrity of the most blessed and most glorious, and ever virgin, Mary, and to the whole body of all the saints, be eternal praise, honour, power, and glory, from every creature, and to us the remission of all sins, through the infinite ages of ages. Amen.'

Surely a very undisguised polytheism this! The prayer is introduced by the following words:—

'*Orationem sequentem devote post Officium recitantibus Leo Papa X. defectus et culpas in eo persolvendo ex humana fragilitate contractas indulsit.*

'SACROSANCTÆ et indíviduæ Trinitáti, crucifixi Dómini nostri Jesu Christi humanitáti, beatíssimæ et gloriosíssimæ, sempérque vírginis Maríæ fœcundæ integritáti, et ómnium Sanctórum universitáti, sit sempitérna laus, honor, virtus et glória ab omni creatúra, nobísque remissio ómnium peccatórum, per infiníta sæcula sæculórum. Amen.'

Be it observed that – (1) No higher terms or formula of worship can be found than 'sit sempitérna laus, honor, virtus et glória ab omni creatúra, per infiníta sæcula sæculórum,' addressed to 'the Virgin Mary, and to the whole body of all the saints.' (2) These terms of worship are addressed *in the same breath*, to 'the most holy and undivided Trinity,' *and* to 'the Virgin Mary, and the whole body of all the saints.' The reader may recall to mind *Rev* 5:13, 'And every creature which is in heaven, and on the earth,' etc., 'heard I saying, Blessing, and honour, and glory, and power, be unto him that sitteth upon the throne, and unto the Lamb for ever and ever.' (3) This thing is not done in a corner. Not only does the prayer occupy a ry prominent place at the beginning of each of the four parts of the Breviary, not only is it prescribed for constant use in connection with its Offices, but, (4) To secure the use of it the more effectually, it is prefaced with the assurance, printed by Rome in emphatic italics, that 'to those devoutly reciting the following prayer after the Office, Pope Leo X. hath granted indulgence of defects and faults contracted through human frailty in the performance thereof!'

At first view, it might possibly seem as if the apostle John's account of the antichrist, in his first Epistle, were but doubtfully applicable to the Papacy, 'He is antichrist, that denieth the Father and the Son'. But Rome, only the more effectually, in some respects, 'denieth the Father and the Son', by professing to believe in both, yet, in connection with both, corrupting and vitiating the whole idea of Divinity. If Popery, like Atheism, disowned a God, or, like Socinianism, openly rejected the divinity and atonement of the Son, then would it be as *weak* at least, as these systems are found to be practically with the mass of mankind. But 'antichrist denieth the Father and the Son' in a more effectual manner; if not by bringing the Father down to the level of the creatures, yet by bringing the creatures up towards his level; and, if not by expressly disowning the deity and atonement of the Son, by conjoining more plausibly endless atonements, priests, mediators, demigods, with his Person and office.

How interesting and instructive to observe, in conclusion, that, however remote from each other Romanism and Socinianism might seem at first view to be, they yet meet in one grand common error lying at the root of both – even *low thoughts of the adorable God – blindness to the alone majesty and glory of Jehovah, as in relation to the creatures of his hand.* Here Arianism, Popery, Socinianism, differing very widely in other respects, meet and agree. And from the same fatal root, of low and debasing thoughts of the one glorious God, spring also heathen Polytheism, heathen (as well as Romish) Image-worship, philosophic Pantheism, and proud Hero-worship, which, all, are but so many different forms of the same frightful error – the Creator confounded with his own creatures, in place of standing quite alone and unapproached, in respect of the highest and meanest of them alike, the 'I AM THAT I AM'. In our next and last chapter it will appear, while we look at the bearings of our theme on Christian faith and life, that there are yet other forms of polytheism and idolatry, springing from the same bitter root of blindness to the glory of the one true and living God, *as wide-spread as there are in the world unconverted and unrenewed men.*

CHAPTER 6

BEARINGS OF THE WHOLE ON CHRISTIAN FAITH AND LIFE.

1. BEARINGS on Christian *faith*. Those incidental testimonies to the Divine glory of Christ which we have found scattered so plenteously over the sacred volume, reach a great deal further, as to their bearing on Christian *faith*, than either the confirming of the truth of our Lord's mission against infidelity, or the confirming of the truth respecting his Person, against such fatal forms of error as Arianism and Socinianism. They will be found to bear vitally also on *the inward saving faith of our Lord Jesus Christ*, on the soul's most inward dealing with all the great objects and grounds of that faith, and more specifically the Saviour's Person, Character and Work.

(1) First, on the dealing of the soul with the glory of the Saviour's *Person*. Need I say how very near the foundation of the whole faith of God's elect lies a living, habitual, realizing apprehension of the *personal* glory of Christ, of the union of the very Godhead and Manhood in the one Mediator between God and men? I am well aware, indeed, of a tendency which has of late appeared, to represent the soul's dealing with Christ as a living *Person*, as almost the only thing of

much consequence to its safety and well-being, and to depreciate correspondingly the importance of just and scriptural thoughts respecting his office and work. But while this is doubtless a very grave error, fraught with manifold and palpable dangers, it is none the less true that the faith which saves the soul, purifies the heart, overcomes the world, has very largely for its object the Person of the Saviour, and does not lie in any mere assent to certain facts regarding him, but very much in the 'beholding of his glory', the trusting of himself, the committing the soul into his hands, as Paul speaks, 'I know whom I have believed, and am persuaded that he is able to keep that which I have committed unto him against that day'; and Peter, 'Lord, to whom shall we go? thou hast the words of eternal life; and we believe and are sure that thou art that Christ, the Son of the living God.' But thus it follows at once, that whatever tends to bring the Person of the Saviour, in its matchless glory, before the eye of the soul, must needs contribute in the same proportion, instrumentally, to lay the foundations, or to lay them deeper, of all genuine faith and religion together. Is it certain, as I have said, that a realizing and habitual apprehension of the glory of Christ as the God-man lies very near the foundation of the whole faith of God's elect? But faith *can* build here only on the inspired word. It is in connection with its devout perusal and meditation alone, that such an apprehension can be either reached or retained. Of what vital importance, then, must it be for that end, if we shall have learned to find this glorious 'mystery of godliness' pervading the Scriptures, and learned to find it, not in those places of them only where it is more nakedly declared, but in the far more numerous ones where it is incidentally taught – taught no less really, and in some respects even more gloriously, though less obviously on the *face* of the inspired record!

(2) As to the bearing of the incidental testimonies on the soul's dealing with Christ in the glory of his *character*, I had occasion to glance at this in the introduction, drawing attention to the fact that the majesty of the Saviour is, in very many of those testimonies, covered over with a certain veil of ineffable gentleness, tenderness, grace, which, however, only renders both the majesty and the gentleness, the greatness and the tenderness, more divinely attractive, so soon as the veil has been lifted up to discover the glory that lies beneath; since it is now not majesty alone, which might alarm, nor gentleness and tenderness alone, which might fail of inspiring reverential and obedient trust, but *both* in a wondrous conjunction, fitted to draw forth at once the confidence and the awe, the submission and the childlike trust, of the weary and sin-laden soul. In place of pursuing this fascinating theme further, however, I venture to refer the reader back to the observations which were there made on it.

(3) Thirdly, under the head of Christian faith, let me glance at the bearing of our incidental testimonies on the soul's dealing with Christ in the glory of his official *work*. It is to be well remembered here, that the faith which saves the soul has for its object, most

characteristically of all, Christ in his *work*, – 'Jesus Christ, and him crucified' – Christ in his whole vicarious obedience unto death. All-glorious as the *incarnation* is, it is not the most central truth of the gospel, – as the ordinance of the Supper, among many other things, demonstrates. Undoubtedly the Lord Jesus intended to embody in that ordinance the very soul of his gospel. It is certain, however, that the leading truth taught in the Supper is, not the incarnation, but the vicarious death, of the Saviour. 'Jesus took bread, and brake it, and gave it to the disciples, saying, Take, eat; this is my body, *broken for you*; this is *my blood, shed for many, for the remission of sins.*' 'As often,' his Apostle adds, 'as ye eat this bread, and drink this cup, ye do shew the Lord's *death* till he come.' True, it is *the Lord's* death. Of what avail for us miserable sinners could the death of any mere creature be? But then, specifically, it is *the death* of the Lord, not his incarnation. They tell us, and rightly, that we have to deal, not with mere doctrines, but with a true and living Person. And, assuredly, it were a fatal error to deal with any doctrines whatsoever, apart from the living Person of the Saviour. But no less fatal were it to deal with the Person, apart from that one only character, office, work, in virtue of which the Son of the living God could be a Saviour for us guilty men. But, now, how vitally important must it needs be for the whole dealing of the soul with this blessed and glorious object, Christ in his Work, if ever, as we trace the pages of the gospel history, from the birth at Bethlehem onwards to the death on Calvary, we shall have learned to behold – not as by some process of reasoning or reflection merely, because we know it otherwise, but directly, and as finding it at almost every step – in the crucified One, the very God-man, Emmanuel, the man that is Jehovah's 'fellow', 'the glory as of the only Begotten of the Father', God over all, blessed for ever! Thus, how shall the whole infinite worth and dignity of the Godhead be seen passing down, as it were, from the Person to the obedience and death, irradiating the entire work, each act of the obedience, the whole sufferings also, blood, curse, death, as being verily His who in our nature is the 'I AM', 'the first and the last and the living One, who was dead, and is alive again, and liveth for evermore!' What a foundation this for a poor soul to build on! What a rock to find beneath our feet! 'Thus saith the Lord God, Behold, I lay in Zion for a foundation, a stone, a tried stone, a precious corner stone, a sure foundation: he that believeth shall not be confounded.'

2. Bearings on Christian *life*.

(1) Let me recall here one of the passages which were made use of in our first chapter as indirect testimonies to the Divine glory of Christ from the claims of his authority, namely, 2 *Cor* 15:14, 15, 'The love of Christ constraineth us; because we thus judge, that if one died for all, then all died: and that he died for all, that they which live should not henceforth *live unto themselves, but unto him who died for them, and rose again.*' With respect to the Divinity of Christ, I thus reasoned from this passage. *To live to* any Being is the

highest worship that can possibly be rendered to him. We are commanded to *live to Christ*, taking his will for our highest law, and himself for our highest end of existence. After this, the mere bowing of the knee is comparatively nothing. If we 'live to Christ', no further or higher worship can remain to be given to Jehovah – if *he* be not Jehovah; and so the entire Scripture doctrine of the Divine unity – especially considered as importing an absolute soleness of glory, quite unapproached and unapproachable, equally absolute in respect of the highest and the meanest of creatures – falls necessarily to the ground.

Well; but there is another aspect of the Apostle's words which I have in view at present: 'that they which live,' he says, 'should not *henceforth live unto themselves*, but', etc. That is to say, he affirms that up till the hour of their union to the Lord Jesus, they *had* 'lived unto themselves,' and given to themselves this highest of all possible real worship. The mere bowing of the knee. I repeat, is comparatively nothing. That is worship, 'My son, give me thine heart', thyself. Ah! it is now no longer the heathen merely. *Thou art the man*, O unconverted reader, 'living unto thyself' at this hour; thine own will, not God's, thy highest law; thyself, not God, thy highest end! The inspired apostle declares – he assumes it as a most certain thing – that thou *livest to thyself*; that we do, all of us, up till the hour of our union with the glorious Saviour, *live unto ourselves* – 'that they who live,' he says, 'should not *henceforth* live unto themselves.'

Oh the frightful guilt of this, as seen in the light of

the absolute soleness of Jehovah's glory, that infinite chasm which subsists between him and all creatures whatsoever! We live by nature to ourselves, both negatively and positively. Negatively; we do *not* live to God. We fail to take his will for our law, himself for our end. As regards the main current of our thoughts, feelings, actions, God is really so very little in them, that it would not make a very great alteration were it to be ascertained that there is not a God at all! 'We do not hate God', is the thought of the natural mind, simply because it hardly comes into any kind of conscious dealing with him. 'We do not *hate* God; we only forget him.' Ah, forget, *only* forget, the 'I AM', besides whom there is, in a sense, no other Being in the universe!

Suppose that a man's father were lying in distress not far off from him, and he should say, Oh, I forgot him – only forgot him! Wretch, we should cry, only forgot thy father! 'We *only* forget God', only rob God of our heart, time, talents, property, family; that is all! But *positively* also we 'live to ourselves'. We transfer from God to ourselves the esteem, the confidence, the fear, the love, the service, which are due only to him. After Paul had thus spoken of the heathen, 'Professing themselves to be wise, they became fools, and changed the glory of the uncorruptible God into an image made like to corruptible man, and to birds, and four-footed beasts, and creeping things,' he adds, 'who changed the truth of God into a lie, and worshipped and served *the creature* more than the Creator, who is blessed for ever.' Worshipped and served *the creature*! But thus are we all in the apostle's charge, since we do by nature 'live unto ourselves'. Yea, in this worship of the creature, we are in some important respects worse than the heathen. For the creatures they worship are sinless at least, however low and mean – those 'birds, and fourfooted beasts, and creeping things'. But we worship our miserably sinful selves. And they, besides, know no better, and might allege also that they look up through the creatures to the unseen God. But we make no such profession in the worship of *ourselves*; and we have the holy Scriptures in our hands, together with a sufficiently orthodox creed framed out of them!

(2) But again, and in intimate connection with this, what light is thus cast over *the evil of sin of every kind*, and *the fearfulness of 'the wrath of God*, revealed from heaven against all ungodliness and unrighteousness of men'! As to sin, and the exceeding evil of it, let those words of Scripture be well noted (*Ps* 51:4), '*Against thee, thee only, have I sinned*, and done evil in thy sight; that thou mightest be justified when thou speakest, and be clear when thou judgest.' Against thee *only*? That the sin of idol-worship, or any other form of express *ungodliness*, should be so written of, it is not difficult to understand. But how does David come so to speak of *his* sin, which, more directly and immediately at least, had so very much to do with men – 'against thee, thee only, have I sinned'? I doubt not that, partly, indeed, the explanation is to be found in this, that sin, *as it is sin*, has to do with God only, being in the essential nature of it, 'the transgression of his law'. While crime is committed against the State, vice

against Society, scandal against the Church, sin, as such, has to do with God. But I have as little doubt that, in David's words, 'against thee only', we have just another of those *onlies*, of which we have already found so many in the Scriptures, with relation to the adorable God. There were, of course, different parties concerned somehow with David's sin. He had in various ways to do with his fellow-men in connection with it. And had he been an unconverted man, a man untaught by the Holy Ghost, doubtless he would have thought of all possible parties in reference to it rather than God, just as we see men, and have too well known ourselves, alas, living for years in sin, and scarcely once thinking of God in connection with it, until the sin perhaps came to take some form in which it met the eyes of men, and threatened us possibly with temporal ruin. Then did we begin for the first time to think somewhat of *God* also in reference to it, though even then much more of man. But what a contrast is here, 'Against *thee, thee only*, have I sinned!' The thought of all others is swallowed up in the consideration of the alone glory, authority, majesty, of 'him with whom we have to do'. *Against thee only* – as if David had said, O Lord, I have sinned against the authority of thy *law*, wherein thou saidst to me thy creature, Thou shalt; but I madly and wickedly said, I will not. I have sinned against thy glorious *character* – against thy power, defying it; thy holiness, dishonouring it; thy wisdom, counting it but folly; thy truth, pronouncing it a lie; thy goodness, preferring my own lusts before it. I have sinned against thy *government* – the only safeguard of the universe. Yea, 'against *thee*', Lord, I have sinned, against thy very being and life, which are wholly inseparable from thy law, thy perfections, thy government. Had my sin been suffered to have its own way, thou hadst been God no more. Oh the infinite evil of sin, as it appears in the light of that name, the 'I AM', as it is beheld directing its aim 'against God, God only!'

But no less is Jehovah alone in his holy *wrath*, revealed from heaven against all ungodliness and unrighteousness of men. 'Who knoweth the power of thine anger?' asks the Psalmist; and he adds, 'even *according to thy fear*, so is thy wrath,'; according, that is to say, to thine own adorable nature, thy power, majesty, burning holiness. True, indeed, the Divine wrath is no *passion*. But very far from being less a reality on that account, it is on that account an unspeakably more dreadful reality. It is no passion, expending itself, like the wrath of man, all the sooner and the more surely, for the very violence of it. It is a fixed principle of the Divine nature; it is the eternal rectitude of that nature, engaged against sin and sinners. 'The LORD thy God *is a consuming fire*', we read in *Deut* 4:24, and again in *Heb* 12:29, where Paul is evidently citing the words of the Pentateuch. Two things come out here. First, that punitive justice belongs essentially to the nature of God. 'Thy God is a consuming fire.' If he might possibly divest himself of what he *has* merely, assuredly he cannot divest himself of what he *is*, without ceasing to be God: but he '*is* a consuming fire'. And then, second, it follows that the *exercise* of the Divine punitive justice, sin being presupposed, is *necessary*. It is not a matter of choice or option with the Lord (to speak with profound reverence), but is of moral necessity by virtue of his very nature, even as it is the nature of *fire* to consume and burn unavoidably whatsoever combustible material it comes in contact with. Sin, the sinner, is the material here, the fuel; and, 'the Lord thy God is a consuming fire'. Oh, well, surely, might the Apostle, in the same chapter where he cites the words from Deuteronomy, say, 'It is a fearful thing to fall into the hands of the living God.' And well may that old and thrilling inquiry be wrung from our innermost hearts, 'Behold the fire and the wood; but *where is the lamb for a burnt offering?*'

(3) But now, finally, what blessed light does our theme cast on the all-glorious answer to that inquiry, 'Behold the Lamb of God, which taketh away the sin of the world!' If, indeed, we should suppose the inquiry to have come from one of the holy angels, looking on with profoundly benevolent interest, beholding man joined to the lost angels in their sin, and so shut up, as it must needs have seemed, to share with them also in their punishment; longing, indeed, if any way of righteous deliverance might be found, and yet shrinking from all thought of the salvation even of a world at the expense of the character of God, the inquiry must necessarily have seemed hopeless of an answer. But here too are God's thoughts and ways beheld high above those of the most exalted creatures, as the heavens are higher than the earth. For if it be so

in very deed, that he who died on the accursed tree, 'the just for the unjust', is none other than the 'I AM', of whose infinite glory we have sought to speak a little, then who shall set any limits to the efficacy of His atoning blood and vicarious righteousness? What a glory then at once irradiates all words like those, 'He is able to save to the uttermost'; 'Deliver from going down to the pit, I have found a ransom'; 'The blood of Jesus Christ, his Son, cleanseth us from all sin'; 'God purchased the Church with his own blood'; 'Awake, O sword, against my shepherd, and against the man that is my fellow, saith the LORD of hosts; smite the shepherd'; 'Christ hath redeemed us from the curse of the law, being made a curse for us'; 'He hath made him to be sin for us, who knew no sin; that we might be made the righteousness of God in him'; 'Reach hither thy finger, and behold my hands; and reach hither thy hand, and thrust it into my side: and be not faithless, but believing. Thomas answered and said unto him, My Lord and my God!'

True, tears will avail nothing here – not oceans of tears – to wipe out *a single sin* against this glorious God. And, if it belong to the very nature of his holiness and justice to consume and burn up sin and sinners, and I am a sinner, then my salvation might well seem a thing impossible. But 'the things which are impossible with men are possible with God.' Jesus, the Son of the living God in our nature, *becomes the burnt offering*, enters into the fire of the Divine wrath, the flames of which break forth against 'the Just One', 'made sin', 'made a curse'. And now – marvellous

gospel of the grace of God! – we are invited to take at
the Father's hand, Christ, instead of hell – Christ free,
instead of hell deserved. 'Oh the depth of the riches
both of the wisdom and knowledge of God! how
unsearchable are his judgments, and his ways past
finding out! For of him, and through him, and to him,
are all things: to whom be glory for ever.'*

With three or four reflections I bring these pages to
a close.

1. How unutterably great is the salvation of the
gospel, of that covenant of grace in which Jehovah, the
all-glorious 'I AM', makes *himself* over to his poor
people, to be their God, portion, husband, everlasting
inheritance, saying, 'I will betroth thee unto me for
ever'; 'thy Maker is thy husband, the LORD of hosts is
his name'; 'I am thy shield, and thine exceeding great
reward'; while the Church is taught to respond, 'The
LORD is the portion of mine inheritance, and of my

---

*I have just used some words of a much loved and valued friend,
to whose intercourse, for a period of more than thirty years, I am
indebted for benefits greater than I can express. Dr John Duncan,
of the New College, Edinburgh, in the course of conversation with
a lady, addressed these remarkable words to her: 'It's a *grand* thing
to begin at the beginning, to begin with the Lord as our maker,
and to learn who and what He is, Jehovah, I am; and then to learn
of him as the Lawgiver; and then to meet him as a Judge, and to
be reconciled to his holy law, – to hear him pronounce the curse
that we deserve, and to say Amen to it; and then to lie at his feet,
confessing that hell is our due, and, lying there, to take at his own
hand, Christ, instead of hell, – Christ free, instead of hell deserved.
That's just salvation, and no way but that will do for you or me.
Try to get it fresh on your conscience every day, that hell is your
desert, and that you take Christ instead.'

cup;' 'thou art my portion, O Jehovah'; 'this God is
our God for ever and ever' 'Behold, what manner of
love the Father hath bestowed on us, that we should
be called the sons of God'; 'and if children, then heirs;
heirs of God, and joint-heirs with Christ'. Of course,
whatsoever blessedness such a God *can* bestow on his
people is thus infallibly secured to them. I believe that
to be the argument of our Lord against the Sadducees
for the resurrection of the body, in the words, 'As
touching the resurrection of the dead, have ye not read
that which was spoken unto you by God, saying, I am
the God of Abraham, and the God of Isaac, and the
God of Jacob?' The argument does not, I apprehend,
lie in the use of the present tense, 'I *am* the God', etc.
Certainly this could prove very little as to the final
resurrection of the bodies of Abraham and Isaac and
Jacob. But it lies, as to soul and body both, in the
substance of the grand covenant promise and relationship, 'I am the *God of* Abraham, and the *God of* Isaac,
and the *God of* Jacob.' As if Jehovah had said, I made
myself over to these men, to be their everlasting
portion; and so, if I am *able* to give eternal life to them,
in soul and body both, no doubt I will do it! 'As
touching the resurrection of the dead, have ye not read
that which was spoken unto you by God, saying, I am
the God of Abraham, and the God of Isaac, and the
God of Jacob. God is not the God of the dead, but of
the living.' Compare those words of the prophet
Habakkuk, 'Art thou not from everlasting, O LORD my
God, mine Holy One? *we shall not die*': and those of
Paul in Hebrews, respecting the certainty and glory of

[92]

the whole eternal blessedness of the saints, 'God is not ashamed to be called *their God*; for he hath prepared for them a city.'

2. How does it become us to be swallowed up with profound awe and self-abasement, as often as we think of the unutterable glory of Jehovah, in connection with our own littleness as creatures, our vileness as creatures sinful, and our infinite obligations to Divine mercy, as redeemed and saved! 'In the year that king Uzziah died, I saw also the Lord sitting upon a throne, high and lifted up, and his train filled the temple. Above it stood the seraphim: each one had six wings; with twain he covered his face, and with twain he covered his feet, and with twain he did fly. And one cried unto another, and said, Holy, holy, holy, is the LORD of hosts; the whole earth is full of his glory. And the posts of the door moved at the voice of him that cried, and the house was filled with smoke. Then said I, Woe is me! for I am undone; because I am a man of unclean lips, and I dwell in the midst of a people of unclean lips; for mine eyes have seen the King, the LORD of hosts'. 'The LORD passed by, and proclaimed, The LORD, The LORD God, merciful and gracious, long-suffering, and abundant in goodness and truth, keeping mercy for thousands, forgiving iniquity and transgression and sin, and that will by no means clear the guilty; visiting the iniquity of the fathers upon the children, and upon the children's children, unto the third and fourth generation. And Moses made haste, and bowed his head toward the earth, and worshipped. And he said, If now I have found grace in thy sight, O Lord, let my

Lord, I pray thee, go among us; for it is a stiffnecked people; and pardon our iniquity and our sin, and take us for thine inheritance'. 'I will praise thee, O LORD my God, with all my heart; and I will glorify thy name for evermore: for great is thy mercy toward me; and thou hast delivered my soul from the lowest hell.'

3. How high the importance of possessing, retaining, and cherishing conceptions of God corresponding in some measure to his infinite glory, excellencies and perfections – thoughts like those of David when he exclaimed, 'Thine, O Jehovah, is the greatness, and the power, and the glory, and the victory, and the majesty'; and of the apostles, in many such words as these: 'Of him, and through him, and to him, are all things'; 'to the only wise God our Saviour, be glory and majesty, dominion and power, both now and ever!' In a former chapter we saw that low thoughts of God are the common poisoned root of all those different forms of doctrinal error – Arianism, Socianism, Romanist and heathen Idolatry, and Pantheism. And now we have seen the same bitter root lying at the bottom of the whole of our own practical idolatry, worship of the creature in its manifold shapes, and, indeed, sin of every kind.

4. And thus, finally, what need to cry ever for the efficacious teaching of the Holy Ghost, for the making good to us of that promise of the new covenant, 'they shall be all taught of God; 'they shall all know me, from the least of them unto the greatest of them'; 'I will give them an heart to know me, that I am Jehovah'. O Lord, be it unto me as thou hast said! Open mine

eyes, that I may behold wondrous things out of thy law! I beseech thee, shew me thy glory! 'We know that the Son of God is come, and hath given us an understanding that we may know him that is true: and we are in him that is true, even in his Son Jesus Christ. This is the true God, and eternal life. Little children, keep yourselves from idols. Amen.'